Gorilla Tag Adventures

Forest Escape

Skibidi McMonke

DEDICATION

To my crew in Gorilla Tag—
The ones who taught me how to pinch climb, wall
jump, and laugh until my headset fogged up. This book
is for the dreamers, the climbers, and the ones who
never give up—even when the ground turns to
quicksand and the Hackers seem unbeatable.

To the readers—
Whether you're a pro branching master or still
mastering your first jump, this adventure is yours too.
Stick together, have fun, and always go bananas.

— Skibidi McMonke

Forest Escape

CONTENTS

Forest Escape

ACKNOWLEDGMENTS

Writing *Gorilla Tag Adventures: Forest Escape* has been an incredible journey, and I couldn't have done it without the amazing support, inspiration, and good vibes from so many people.

To my *real-life crew*—you know who you are—thank you for always being up for a round of Gorilla Tag and for sharing your epic moves, hilarious fails, and contagious laughter. This book wouldn't exist without you. You're the reason this game feels more like a second home than just a virtual world.

To the *Gorilla Tag community*—thank you for the memes, the jokes, and the moments of chaos that make every game unforgettable. You're a never-ending source of inspiration. Whether you're pinch climbing to the moon, rocking banana drip, or playing hide-and-seek in the caves, you make Gorilla Tag the unique experience it is.

A huge shoutout to my alter ego, *Skibidi McMonke*. You bring the humor, heart, and occasional silliness that every Gorilla Tag adventure needs. This book's jokes, thrills, and monke shenanigans are all thanks to you.

To *you*, the reader—you're the true star of this journey. Whether you're a Gorilla Tag veteran or just curious about this wacky virtual jungle, thank you for taking this adventure with me. You're the heart of the *Gorilla Tag Adventures* series, and every page is for you.

And hey, don't forget—this is just the beginning. Keep those VR headsets charged, because there's so much more ahead in the *Gorilla Tag Adventures* series. See you on the Maps!

– Skibidi McMonke 🦍 🌿

Forest Escape

PROLOGUE

The sun was peeking through the lush canopy of the Forest map, casting dappled patches of light across the ground. Towering trees stretched high into the virtual sky, their thick trunks perfect for climbing and hiding. The air inviting with the sound of stirring leaves as a gentle breeze swept through, carrying the faint echoes of chirping birds that seemed to cheer on the players. The atmosphere was alive with energy—like the jungle itself was buzzing with anticipation, waiting for the first move.

In the middle of it all stood the iconic central tree, a massive giant that rose above everything else. Its branches spread wide like open arms, inviting players to swing, climb, and leap from its sturdy limbs. Around the base of the tree, wooden platforms formed a makeshift playground, interconnected by bridges and ramps. They were a perfect spot for strategizing, playing tag, or simply catching a breath before diving back into the action.

This was the crew's favorite spot in Gorilla Tag—a place they'd come to know like the back of their hand.

Today, they were meeting up in their private room, named "ArmsUp," a little inside joke from when they first started playing. Back then, they barely knew how to move without crashing into the ground, but now they were ready for anything the game threw at them. Well, almost anything.

The sound of branches creaking gave away the first sign of movement. A shadow zipped across the ground, quickly followed by the echo of laughter. It was going to be another wild day in the Forest, and the group was eager to get started, swinging from branch to branch like real-life monkeys. Here, among the leafy green shade and the familiar trails, their adventure was just beginning.

The group swung into view, arms pumping as they vaulted from one tree branch to another. The air filled with the sound of laughter, playful shouts, and the slap of virtual hands hitting wood. Today wasn't just another game; it was their first meetup in the private room. It was a place where they could be themselves—no other players, no interruptions. Just friends, fun, and a whole lot of monkey business.

"Race you to the top of the big tree!" shouted Cooked, the orange-colored daredevil of the group. He was already halfway up the trunk, moving with his usual fearless speed. "Last one there is a noob!"

"Cooked, you're always showing off," Tactix, the green strategist, called up from below. He wasn't racing—he was analyzing. Tactix scanned the branches, mapping out the fastest route in his head. "If you go left, you're going to get stuck. Watch out for that gap!"

"Yeah, yeah, Mr. Brainiac. You think too much!" Cooked laughed, swinging wide across a branch and nearly losing his grip. He twisted mid-air, managing to land on the next platform with a whoop. "See? I've got this!"

"You've got something all right," joked ClassClown, the dark blue jokester of the group. He was hanging from a low branch, pretending to struggle. "Help! I'm stuck! Oh no, I guess I'm going to fall right into that picnic basket full of bananas."

"Classic ClassClown," chuckled Swizzler, the versatile red gorilla. He was perched calmly on a narrow branch above, balancing on one hand like it was the easiest thing in the world. "You know, if you spent as much time practicing as you do goofing off, you might actually be decent at this game."

"Hey, my job is to make you all laugh," ClassClown grinned. "And I'm the best at it. No cap."

"Focus, guys!" shouted Trekka, the white explorer of the group. She was already scouting the higher branches, peering into the distance. "There's a hidden tunnel over there we haven't explored yet."

"You always find the secret stuff, Trekka," said Griddy, the purple-colored kind-hearted friend who never gave up, even when she struggled. She was hanging back, trying to master the wall jump with a look of intense concentration on her face. "I'm still just trying to get the hang of climbing without slipping."

"You're getting better, Griddy!" Swizzler called down, swinging over to help. "Remember, it's all in the wrist motion. Like this."

"You guys make it look so easy," Griddy huffed, but she smiled. "But I'll get there. Just watch me!"

The banter flowed easily between them, a rhythm they'd developed over countless games together. They weren't just teammates—they were a crew, each with their own style and strengths. They knew each other from school, but it was Gorilla Tag that had cemented their bond. It wasn't long before they made ArmsUp their go-to hangout, where they could practice, laugh, and push each other to get better.

Just as they were settling into their usual routine, the game's atmosphere shifted. The birds stopped chirping, and the usual rustle of leaves faded into an unnatural stillness. It felt like the Forest itself was waiting, tense and alert. From the shadows, a figure zipped across the ground—a flash of black darting through the trees.

"Did you guys see that?" Tactix asked, squinting into the darkness. He dropped to the ground, signaling for the group to regroup. "Something's not right. We're the only ones who should be in here."

"I thought this was a private room," Cooked said, dropping down beside him with a frown. "Who could've gotten in?"

"Maybe it's just a glitch," Swizzler said, but his voice sounded uncertain. "Or maybe… someone let them in."

ClassClown shifted nervously, avoiding their gaze. He forced a laugh, but it came out shaky. "Uh… I mean, what's the big deal? It's probably nothing. Let's just keep playing."

But they all knew better. The Forest wasn't empty anymore, and the playful mood had suddenly turned serious. Whoever—or whatever—was out there wasn't supposed to be.

And this time, they might be playing a game they weren't ready for.

The world of Gorilla Tag was unlike any other game the group had ever played. There were no legs—just a torso, a head, and long, swinging arms that propelled players through the world. It wasn't about pressing buttons; it was about moving your body. To climb a tree, you had to reach out, grab a trunk with both hands, and pull yourself up with a powerful motion, like you were hoisting yourself out of a pool. Every movement depended on how well you could use your arms. It was all about swinging, gripping, and using momentum to leap from branch to branch.

"Pinch climbing 101," Cooked called out, demonstrating the technique for Griddy. He pressed his virtual hands against the trunk of the central tree, pinching it tightly as he shuffled his hands upward. "It's like grabbing a big cookie. Squeeze it tight and don't let go!"

Griddy gave it a try, managing to climb a few feet before slipping back down to the ground. She laughed, shaking her head. "Well, I'm no cookie monster. More like cookie crumbles."

"You've got this!" encouraged Swizzler. He swung by effortlessly, using his arms like a gymnast on parallel bars. He propelled himself higher, grabbing onto a branch and pulling up into a perfect landing. "It's all about the rhythm. Push, pull, grab, swing."

The air was filled with the sounds of the game: the gentle creak of the tree trunks as they were climbed, the swishing of leaves brushing against the gorillas' bodies, and the sharp pop of a jump as a player launched themselves into the air. Birds chirped overhead, and in the distance, the faint babble of a hidden waterfall could be heard, creating an atmosphere that was both peaceful and full of potential energy.

Suddenly, a new sound sliced through the air—a snap, like a twig breaking under Monke.

Tactix froze, lifting a hand to signal the group. "Did you hear that?" he whispered, eyes sharpening as he scanned the underbrush below.

"Probably just a squirrel," ClassClown said, though his voice wavered slightly. He swung lower, hanging upside down to peer into the forest. "Or maybe it's just my imagination... again."

But the group fell silent, every head turning in the same direction. The leaves rustled, and a shadow moved quickly between the trunks, too fast to be any of them.

"Is it another player?" Trekka asked, her voice dropping to a whisper. She instinctively began to climb higher, seeking a better vantage point.

Cooked's playful grin faded, replaced by a look of intense focus. "No," he muttered, shaking his head slowly. "We're in a private room. It shouldn't be anyone else."

The group exchanged nervous glances. A chill ran through the air, and the once-friendly forest felt different—darker, more secretive. It felt like the entire map was frozen in suspense, waiting for something to happen.

"Everyone, regroup," Tactix ordered quietly. "Whatever it is, it's not here to play nice."

Just as they began to move, the shadow darted again, this time closer—too close. A deep, echoing laugh filled the air, bouncing off the virtual trees, sending shivers down their spines.

"Who's there?" Cooked called out, his voice steady but laced with suspicion.

The only answer was the sound of leaves rustling and a whisper that seemed to come from everywhere and nowhere at once. "You'll find out... soon."

1 MEET THE CREW

The Forest map was filled with the sounds of creaking branches and the laughter of the group, but the echo of that unfamiliar rustling hadn't gone away. It was as if the forest itself was whispering a warning. Cooked landed on a platform halfway up the central tree, pausing for a moment to glance around. His orange torso twisted as he peered into the shadowy spaces between the branches. Nothing.

"Alright, enough with the warm-ups," Cooked called out, shaking off the uneasy feeling. "Who's ready for infection mode? Let's see who's the real tag master today!"

The group gathered below, bouncing on their hands in excitement. Griddy, still panting a little from her practice runs, clapped her purple hands together. "I'm in! Just don't come for me first," she laughed, glancing playfully at Swizzler.

Swizzler grinned, flipping himself onto a branch with ease. "Oh, I wouldn't dream of it, Griddy. I'll save you for last," he teased, winking. "But watch out for Tactix—he's got that 'tag everyone in three moves' strategy ready to go."

Tactix, perched on a high branch, looked down with a smirk. "You know it. And I've got new routes planned, too. No one's escaping me today."

ClassClown rolled his eyes dramatically, his dark blue form slumping in mock defeat. "Great, so I'll be the first one tagged, as usual. Let me get my jokes ready because that's all I'm good for."

Trekka leapt down from a nearby branch, her white hands catching the sunlight. "I call first tag!" she shouted, her voice echoing through the forest as she tapped Cooked on the back. "Tag—you're it!"

Cooked laughed and pushed off the tree, launching himself into the game. "Oh, it's on now!" he called out, as the others scattered in all directions. The forest came alive with the sounds of thumping hands, laughter, and the flutter of leaves as they darted through the branches.

But just as the excitement reached its peak, there was a different sound—a soft, deliberate tap-tap of hands that didn't belong to anyone in their group. The steps were slow, measured, and seemed to come from the far side of the central tree.

Griddy froze for a second, her ears twitching as she listened. "Did you guys hear that?" she whispered, looking around at her friends.

Swizzler, hanging upside down from a branch, tilted his head. "Hear what? The sound of me winning?" he joked, but there was a flicker of uncertainty in his eyes.

"No, seriously," Trekka said, landing beside Griddy. "It sounded like… someone else. But there's only six of us in this room, right?"

Cooked spun around, focusing his eyes as he scanned the treetops. "Yeah, we're the only ones here. It's a private room—ArmsUp—no one else can join unless we invite them."

The group exchanged uneasy glances, their earlier laughter fading as the realization settled in. Tactix was the first to break the silence. "Okay, let's stick together for a minute. We can switch to infection mode in a sec, but first, let's make sure we're alone here."

The leaves rustled above them, and there it was again—the sound of another player's steps, moving quickly and then stopping. It felt like the unseen figure was watching them, waiting.

ClassClown, trying to lighten the mood, grinned nervously. "Maybe it's just the wind… or a ghost monke here to tag us all."

Cooked's face grew serious. "Wind doesn't make footsteps like that. And I've got a feeling this isn't just some glitch."

He glanced up at the shadowy branches above, where the noise had come from. "Alright, crew," he said quietly, his voice low but steady. "Let's keep playing, but stay sharp. I don't think we're alone here."

Without another word, they launched back into the game, but the playful atmosphere had shifted. There was a tension now, an unspoken agreement to watch each other's backs as they swung through the forest. The mysterious sound lingered in the air, building suspense with every passing moment.

Infection mode had begun, but it felt like they were already being hunted by something—or someone—they couldn't see.

The group moved deeper into the forest, still listening for the mysterious sounds. They stuck close together, each one showing off their skills in their own way.

"Alright, if we're doing infection mode, I'm calling dibs on first tag," Cooked declared, leaping effortlessly onto a high branch. He swung from one limb to the next with ease, his orange form darting through the leaves like a flash of fire. "And by the way, you all better be ready—I'm not holding back!"

"Yeah, yeah, Mr. Daredevil," Swizzler called back, his red torso flipping gracefully as he vaulted over a low branch. "Just don't get too cooked yourself up there, buddy. You know what they say: the higher they climb, the harder they fall!"

Cooked laughed. "Hey, I've got this under control. You're just jealous you can't pull off these moves."

Griddy, balancing on a nearby branch, gave a supportive cheer. "You've got this, Cooked! But maybe save a little of that energy for later. You know, when you have to help me get off the ground again." She tried a small jump up the trunk, only to slip back down, landing with a thud. "Oops! Well, at least I'm consistent," she grinned.

ClassClown swung in low, barely managing to hold onto a thin branch. He adjusted his nerd glasses cosmetic, peering up at the others with a cheeky smile. "Consistency is key, Griddy. It's like my consistent noob moves—they never fail to entertain. I'd like to think I'm here for comic relief."

Tactix, the green strategist, landed beside them. He pointed up towards the double walls that led to the top of the central tree. "While you guys are joking around, I'm thinking we use the double wall climb as our main escape route. If we stick together, we can branch out near the top and—"

Trekka cut him off with an excited shout. "Or, we can go through the secret tunnel I found before!" The white explorer monkey's eyes sparkled as she pointed towards a narrow crevice in the cliffside. "It looks tricky, but I can't wait to see where it leads."

Swizzler nodded, impressed. "Good find, Trekka. That's why you're the scout of the group."

"Alright, team," Tactix said, clapping his hands together. "We've got our plan. Now let's—"

He was interrupted by the sudden sound of a loud thud, followed by the unmistakable rhythm of heavy footsteps. They all froze, eyes darting to the shadows above.

ClassClown's voice dropped to a whisper. "Uh, guys... please tell me one of you just fell out of a tree?"

No one answered.

Cooked narrowed his eyes, his voice barely a murmur. "Looks like our mystery guest is back. And this time, they're getting closer."

The group exchanged nervous glances, their playful banter fading as the sense of unease crept back in. Whoever was out there wasn't just watching anymore— they were moving in.

The group took their positions, spreading out among the branches of the central tree. Infection mode was in full force, and the tension kept rising. They could feel the shift in the air—the playful vibe from earlier had turned into focused concentration.

Cooked, perched on a high branch, surveyed the forest below. "Alright, team, stay sharp. Remember the plan: Tactix and Trekka take the double walls, Swizzler covers Griddy, and I'll be on distraction duty."

ClassClown, hanging upside down from a low branch, gave a dramatic salute. "Yes, sir, Captain Cooked! Just don't get too 'cooked' out there!"

The group chuckled, but their laughter was cut short by the sound of swift, heavy footsteps echoing from the shadows. It was different this time—quieter, calculated.

Whoever was out there knew how to stay hidden.

"That's definitely not one of us," Trekka whispered, her eyes wide as she scanned the treetops. "Did anyone else invite a friend?"

Cooked shook his head, his expression serious now. "Nope, just us in the private room. At least, it should be."

Before anyone could respond, a black figure darted out of the shadows, moving faster than they'd ever seen. The group barely had time to react as the dark gorilla, Shadow, zipped past them, tagging Tactix and sending him falling from his spot on the double wall.

Tactix groaned from the ground, shaking his head. "What just happened? Did anyone even see him coming?"

Shadow's sinister laugh echoed through the forest, sending chills down their spines. "Didn't see that one, did you?" he taunted, his voice dripping with amusement. He clung effortlessly to the underside of a thick branch, blending into the shadows as if he were a part of them.

Swizzler's eyes intensified. "It's Shadow. I've heard about him. He's known for using glitches and sneaky tricks to tag players before they even know he's there."

Griddy huddled closer to Trekka, her confidence shaken. "How did he get in here? This was supposed to be our private room."

ClassClown tried to lighten the mood, but his nervous laugh gave him away. "Well, at least we know we've got a VIP guest. Shadow himself—here to tag us noobs!"

Cooked dropped down to ground level, facing Shadow head-on. "Alright, Shadow," he said, his tone daring but steady. "If you're going to crash our game, let's make it interesting. How about a challenge? One-on-one—you and me."

Shadow tilted his head, a smirk evident even without facial features. "Oh, you want to take me on alone, Cooked? That's bold. I've seen your moves—you're fast, but are you clever enough to keep up?"

The group watched in tense silence, holding their breath. They knew this was risky—Cooked was fearless, but Shadow had a reputation for outsmarting even the best players. This was more than just a game now; it was a test of skill, strategy, and who could outmaneuver the other.

"Let's find out," Cooked replied, gripping the nearest trunk with both hands and launching himself up into the trees.

Shadow's laughter faded as he darted after him, leaving the rest of the crew behind, watching the two figures disappear into the canopy above.

Tactix looked at the group, his voice a mix of concern and determination. "We can't just stand here. We need to back him up. Shadow's tricky—we need to be ready when Cooked needs us."

"Agreed," Trekka nodded, already planning a route through the branches. "Let's show Shadow he messed with the wrong crew."

Griddy clenched her fists, a look of fierce determination on her face. "I might not be the best at climbing, but I can still help. Let's go!"

With a final nod of agreement, the group took off into the forest, united and ready to face the challenge ahead.

The crew darted through the forest, their arms swinging with precision as they navigated the maze of branches. The tension was palpable, but so was their determination. They couldn't let Shadow win—especially not after crashing their private room.

Up in the canopy, Cooked was in the heat of it, leaping from branch to branch with Shadow hot on his trail. The two of them were a blur of motion, swinging and juking, their movements almost mirror images.

ClassClown tried to keep up, watching from below. "Is it just me, or do those two look like they're having a dance-off? I mean, if this was a talent show, I'd give them both a solid ten out of ten!"

Tactix smirked, even as he focused on their strategic positioning. "If this is a dance-off, Cooked better pull out his best moves because Shadow's got some serious footwork—well, arm work, technically."

"Less talk, more tagging!" Trekka called out, grabbing a vine and swinging up to the higher branches. She paused, scanning the treetops for any sign of Cooked. "Where are they? I lost sight of them!"

Just then, a loud crack echoed through the forest, followed by a sudden swishing of leaves. Cooked came tumbling down, barely catching himself on a thin branch before he could hit the ground.

"Cooked!" Griddy shouted, worry etched across her face. "Are you okay?"

Cooked dangled there for a second, then grinned, panting heavily. "Never better. Just taking a quick break—hanging around, you know?"

ClassClown burst out laughing. "That was the most graceful fall I've ever seen. Bravo, Cooked! Truly a masterful performance."

But their laughter was cut short as a shadowy figure emerged from the darkness above. Shadow perched silently on a branch, barely visible against the dim foliage, his laugh a low, mocking whisper. "You're good, Cooked. I'll give you that. But you can't outrun the shadows forever."

Cooked swung himself up onto the branch, standing

tall despite his exhaustion. "Maybe not," he admitted, catching his breath. "But I don't have to. I've got my crew."

At that cue, the rest of the team leaped into action, surrounding Shadow from all sides. Tactix pointed out a route, Trekka swung in from the left, and Swizzler zipped in from the right, moving faster than Shadow could anticipate.

For the first time, Shadow hesitated, glancing around at the coordinated effort. "Clever," he muttered. "But this isn't over."

Before they could make a move, Shadow vanished into the leaves, blending seamlessly with the shadows of the forest. He was gone as quickly as he had appeared, leaving the group standing there, panting and wide-eyed.

"Did we just win?" Swizzler asked, looking around in disbelief.

"I don't know," Tactix replied, frowning. "But I have a feeling this isn't the last we'll see of him."

Cooked nodded, wiping the sweat from his brow. "He'll be back. But next time, we'll be ready."

Just as they were about to relax, they heard it—a faint stirring in the distance. This time, it wasn't just footsteps. It was the unmistakable sound of another player climbing up the central tree. The group froze, exchanging nervous glances.

"Who's there?" Trekka called out, her voice echoing through the forest.

There was no answer, just the eerie sound of leaves murmuring and a soft chuckle that wasn't Shadow's.

ClassClown gulped, his usual humor gone. "Uh, guys... I don't think we're alone."

The scene faded out, leaving the forest in silence, save for the distant, creeping sound of someone—or something—approaching.

2 FRIEND OR FOE

The group continues playing in their private room, ArmsUp, still buzzing with the excitement and tension from their encounter with Shadow. They gather at the flat top of the giant central tree stump, which offers a sweeping view of the entire Forest map. The wind stirs through the leaves above them, creating a soothing backdrop of chirping birds and the occasional crack of a branch.

Cooked, brimming with energy and always eager for the next challenge, flashes a confident grin at his friends. "Alright, who's ready to level up? We've got some serious skills to sharpen after that last game. Shadow gave us a run for our money."

Trekka's eyes light up with determination. "I'm ready," she says, bouncing on her toes. "Let's go for double walls again. I've been practicing my jumps, and I think I've almost got it!"

ClassClown rolls his eyes playfully, sliding down the tree trunk with exaggerated, clumsy movements. "Double walls? I can barely handle single walls! Check it out—I'm inventing a new move called 'The Slippery

Banana Slide'!" He flails his arms as he mock-falls, eliciting a chorus of laughter from the group.

Swizzler, ever the supportive teammate, nudges ClassClown with a friendly elbow. "You've got talent— just not for climbing," he teases. "Stick to the comedy; it's your strongest skill."

Griddy, who's been quietly practicing her jumps with a look of fierce concentration, suddenly beams as she finally reaches the lowest branch of the central tree. "Guys, look! I did it! I'm actually up here!"

"You're improving fast, Griddy," Tactix says, nodding in approval as he analyzes the group's progress. "But we can't lose focus. We still don't know if Shadow is hiding somewhere, watching us."

A hush falls over the group as they process Tactix's words. The quivering of leaves, so familiar and comforting a moment ago, now feels ominous. Suddenly, they all hear it—a faint, rhythmic sound of footsteps. It's almost imperceptible, like the wind brushing against the forest floor, but distinct enough to make them freeze in place.

Trekka's voice drops to a whisper as she scans the surrounding darkness. "Did you guys hear that?"

"Yeah," Swizzler replies, his eyes contracting. "And I don't think it's just the wind this time."

They exchange uneasy glances, the playful mood evaporating as the suspense builds. Whoever is making those footsteps is moving closer.

The silver gorilla steps into the clearing, his metallic sheen catching the dappled sunlight. He moves with an effortless grace, landing softly on the ground in front of them, as if he's been here all along, watching them from the edges. The group tenses, still wary after their bizarre encounter with Shadow.

Cooked steps forward, his usual confidence tempered

with caution. "Hey there! We didn't catch your name," he says, offering a small nod of acknowledgment.

The newcomer grins, his eyes glinting mischievously. "Name's Glitch. Judging by the way you're all huddled up like scared little monke's, I'd say you weren't expecting company."

ClassClown, ever the jokester, puts his hands on his hips and smirks. "Huddled? Please, we're just, uh... practicing our synchronized fear dance. It's a new team-building exercise."

The group chuckles, but there's an underlying tension. Griddy, still catching her breath from her climb, blurts out the question everyone's been thinking, "Are you a friend of Shadow? Because our last run-in with him was... well, unexpected."

Glitch's smile widens, but there's a hint of something else behind it—something calculating. He hops effortlessly onto a nearby branch, balancing as if it were second nature. "Shadow? We've crossed paths. He's got skills, I'll give him that. But I'm here for something different. I want to see what you can do."

Tactix pinpoints his eyes, stepping closer to study Glitch. "You don't seem like just another player. What's your game?"

Glitch's expression shifts slightly, a flicker of amusement in his eyes. "Oh, I'm all about pushing limits," he says, swinging from one branch to another with the ease of a CEO. "But from what I've seen, you all could use a few pointers."

Trekka, ever the curious explorer, tilts her head. "Pointers? Like what? We're pretty good at the basics."

"Basics are for beginners," Glitch replies, his voice dropping to a teasing whisper. "You want to go faster? Loosen your grip. Most players cling too tightly, thinking it'll keep them steady. But all it does is slow you down.

You need to trust the swing, use your arms to build momentum."

Swizzler decides to give it a try. Following Glitch's advice, he loosens his grip and swings out from the branch, feeling an unexpected rush of speed. He soars higher than he ever has before, landing gracefully on the next platform. "Whoa, that actually works!" he exclaims, his eyes wide with excitement.

Glitch lands lightly in front of them, watching with an amused expression. "You've got potential, I'll admit that," he says, glancing at each of them in turn. "But you're still playing it too safe. If you want to get better, you'll have to take a few more risks."

Cooked exchanges a look with Tactix, sensing there's more to this new player than meets the eye. "Why are you really here, Glitch?" he asks, his tone now serious. "You didn't just stumble into our private room for a quick tutorial, did you?"

Glitch's grin fades slightly, and for a brief moment, his eyes darken. "Let's just say I have a vested interest in players like you. You're not the only ones looking for answers in the Forest. But those answers don't come for free."

The group falls silent, feeling the weight of Glitch's words. There's a deeper game being played here, and they're only just starting to see the edges of it.

"Alright," Glitch says, clapping his hands together as if shaking off the tension. "Show me what you've got. Let's see if you can keep up."

With a sudden burst of speed, Glitch bolts up the central tree trunk, faster than any of them have ever seen before. It's like he's gliding effortlessly, his silver arms a blur against the bark. The group watches, momentarily stunned—this player isn't just good; he's in a league of his own.

Cooked, always the fearless leader, tapers his eyes and shouts after him. "Let's see if you can handle our crew!"

Tactix jumps into action, his mind racing with strategies. "We need to spread out and use the double walls for height advantage," he orders. "Swizzler, stick with Griddy and help her climb higher. We'll need all the elevation we can get."

Griddy nods, her face set in determination. "I'm ready. Let's do this!" She's been struggling with wall climbing, but this challenge is giving her the motivation she needs.

ClassClown, predictably sliding back down the trunk with exaggerated flailing, calls out, "Don't worry, I'm here for moral support—and comic relief! I'll make sure Glitch laughs too hard to tag us."

The group springs into action, swinging and climbing through the branches as they try to keep pace with Glitch. He moves like a boss, darting between trees, his movements fluid and precise. It's clear he's testing them, showing off a level of skill that leaves even Cooked in awe.

Trekka, always the keen explorer, spots the secret tunnel again—the one she noticed when Shadow disappeared. It's hidden along the right side of the Forest map, a narrow, dark path that seems to lead deeper into unknown territory. "Guys, look!" she shouts. "That tunnel—it's a hidden path! I think it leads somewhere important. It must be where Shadow slipped away last time."

But before they can investigate further, Glitch swings down from above, landing gracefully right in front of the tunnel's entrance. He blocks their path with a playful smirk, like a gatekeeper daring them to make a move. "Not so fast," he says, holding up a hand. "You've got to prove yourselves first."

Cooked steps forward, his expression determined. "What do you have in mind?"

Glitch tilts his head, considering them all for a moment. "Infection Mode," he declares simply. The challenge hangs heavy in the air, signaling a high-stakes game where one infected player must tag everyone else to restart the game with a new infected player. "If you can tag me, I'll show you the secrets of this map," Glitch continues. "But if I tag all of you first... well, let's just say you might end up a little lost in this Forest."

The group exchanges glances, a mix of excitement and nerves in their expressions. Swizzler flexes his fingers, ready for a new challenge. Tactix starts mapping out escape routes in his mind. Griddy takes a deep breath, trying to shake off her nerves, while Trekka's eyes sparkle with anticipation at the thought of discovering new secrets.

"You're on," Cooked replies confidently, stepping into the clearing. He knows his crew has what it takes—they've faced tough players before, but this feels different. Glitch isn't just another player; he's a puzzle they have to solve, a test of everything they've learned so far.

"Alright then," Glitch says, giving a small bow. "Let the game begin."

With that, he bolts up the nearest tree, disappearing into the thick canopy. The group scatters, ready for the chase. The sound of leaves ruffling and branches snapping fills the air as they leap into action. But somewhere in the back of their minds, they can't help but wonder—what's Glitch really after, and why does he know so much about the hidden paths of the Forest?

It's a question they'll have to answer quickly because the game has only just begun.

The game switches to Infection Mode, and the

atmosphere shifts. Everyone feels the intensity rise as Glitch starts as the first infected player. He flashes a confident grin before darting into the treetops, his movements a blur. The group exchanges determined looks—they're ready for this.

Tactix takes the lead, directing his friends like a commander. "Use the double walls for speed!" he shouts. "Swizzler, help Griddy climb higher—she's improving every second!"

Fueled by the encouragement, Griddy digs deep, pushing past her usual hesitation. She pulls herself up, gripping tightly, and makes it to the highest branch she's ever reached. Her voice rings out, filled with joy and disbelief. "I did it! I'm actually up here!"

Glitch, the tagger, swings effortlessly through the trees, his movements a blur of precision. Cooked, always ready for a challenge, takes a daring leap from the top of the central tree. He soars through the air, aiming to outmaneuver Glitch. At the last second, Glitch pivots and flips, with perfect timing to avoid Cooked's attempt. Cooked lands in a smooth roll, popping back up with a grin. 'You're quick, I'll give you that,' he laughs, his competitive spirit shining through.

ClassClown swings wildly through the branches, nearly colliding with Swizzler. "Maybe we should just ask Glitch for a cheat code!" he jokes, making the group laugh despite the tension.

Glitch moves like a ghost, slipping through the branches and making impossible turns. He surprises Trekka, who had been busy exploring the edges of the map. With a quick tap, she's tagged. "Nice try," Glitch says with a playful wink. "But you'll have to be faster next time."

Trekka isn't discouraged—if anything, she's more excited. "Oh, there will be a next time," she replies, her eyes gleaming with determination.

As the game winds down, the group catches their breath, regrouping in the clearing. Glitch lands softly in front of them, looking impressed. "You guys aren't half bad," he admits. "Maybe I'll stick around for a while."

Cooked steps forward, offering a fist bump. "We could use a rival like you," he says. There's a new spark of camaraderie in the air—a mix of respect and friendly competition.

But before they can say more, the sound of distant footsteps echoes through the Forest once again. This time, it's different. Heavier. More deliberate. It's not just the light crackle of leaves; it's the kind of sound that sends a shiver down your spine.

Swizzler's eyes widen as he glances around nervously. "Uh, guys?" he whispers. "I think we've got more company."

Glitch tilts his head towards the shadows, a smirk forming on his lips. "Guess the fun isn't over yet," he says, his voice low and excited. "Hope you're all warmed up, because it's about to get wild."

The group turns toward the deeper shadows of the Forest, where the sound of footsteps is growing louder. It's as if the trees themselves are holding a secret, waiting for what comes next.

And just like that, the game isn't over—it's only just beginning.

3 INFECTION MODE

The sun filters through the treetops, casting dancing shadows across the Forest map. The air is vibrating with a mix of excitement and tension as the group gears up for their next official round of Infection Mode with their new rival, Glitch. The distant sound of birdsong contrasts with the heavy thudding of gorilla hands pounding against the wooden platforms and tree trunks. The atmosphere is electric.

Cooked takes a deep breath, feeling the rush of adrenaline. "Alright, Infection Mode it is. Glitch starts as the infected," he announces. The group spreads out immediately, each player darting off in different directions. Trekka swings up to a high branch, Tactix heads for the double walls, and Swizzler leads Griddy towards a safer spot to practice her jumps.

"Stick together and use the trees for cover!" Tactix calls out, already scanning the area for strategic routes. He's in his element, formulating a plan on the fly. "If we spread out too far, we'll be easy targets."

Griddy, trying her best to keep up, stumbles a bit but quickly regains her footing. "I've got this!" she says, her voice filled with determination. She takes a deep breath and leaps, managing to grab a higher branch. It's a small victory, but one that boosts her confidence.

In the distance, Glitch starts to move, his silver sheen flashing in the sunlight as he bolts up the central tree. The group can hear his laughter echoing through the forest. "Ready or not, here I come!" he shouts, his voice filled with playful mischief.

ClassClown, hanging upside down from a branch, grins. "Well, this should be fun. I hope Glitch is ready for some Grade-A comic relief!" He wiggles his arms in mock terror, making the others laugh despite the tension.

The footsteps grow louder as Glitch draws closer, his movements swift and calculated. The game is on, and the group knows they'll need to bring their A-game if they want to outsmart their mysterious new rival.

"Let's show him what we've got," Cooked says, his voice filled with confidence as he makes eye contact with each of his friends. The energy is intense, and the stage is set for an epic showdown.

The sound of branches swishing fills the air as they scatter, with Glitch's shadow looming larger and larger in the background.

The group is deep into their Infection Mode game, laughing and swinging from branch to branch. The camaraderie is profound—until a loud, mocking voice interrupts their fun.

"Well, well, well, look who we have here—a bunch of wannabe monke's!" A dark blue gorilla with a flashy name tag reading "Cringe" drops down in front of them, blocking their path. His grin is wide and insincere, the kind that immediately makes everyone uneasy.

ClassClown's usual smile fades as he whispers to Cooked, "Oh great, it's Cringe. This guy lives to ruin everyone's game."

Cooked tries to keep the energy light. "Hey, Cringe. We're just here to have a good time. Why don't you join in instead of trash-talking?"

Cringe snorts, swinging up to a higher branch to loom over them. "Join you? Nah, I'd rather watch you all embarrass yourselves. It's way more entertaining." He points at Griddy, who's nervously trying to climb. "Look at her! Can't even make it up the first branch. Pathetic."

Griddy flinches at his words but takes a deep breath. "I'm just practicing. Everyone starts somewhere, right?"

"Practicing?" Cringe mimics her voice in a mocking tone. "More like failing. If I were as bad as you, I'd uninstall the game."

Trekka, swinging close to defend her friend, glares at Cringe. "Back off. We're all here to get better and have fun. What's your problem?"

Cringe laughs, a harsh sound that echoes through the Forest. "My problem? My problem is noobs like you clogging up the servers. You're not even worth tagging—too easy."

Swizzler steps in, his tone calm but firm. "Just leave us alone, Cringe. There's no need to be like this."

"Oh, I get it," Cringe says with a smirk. "The little squad of losers is sticking together. How cute. You think teamwork is going to save you?"

Tactix focuses his eyes, his strategic mind already working on a plan. "We've dealt with players like you before, Cringe. You think bullying us makes you look strong, but it just shows everyone how weak you really are."

Cringe's grin falters for a second before he recovers. He swings down to stand right in front of Tactix, towering over him. "Watch it, brainiac. You might be good with strategy, but I'm good at ruining games. And if you push me, I'll make sure you never want to play again."

The atmosphere grows tense as the group huddles closer. Even Glitch, who's been watching quietly from a nearby branch, seems to sense the shift.

ClassClown tries to defuse the situation with humor, as always. "Hey, Cringe, why don't you take a break? Maybe grab a banana—sounds like you need a snack."

Cringe steps closer, his voice dropping to a threatening whisper. "You think this is funny, clown? Keep joking, and I'll make sure you're tagged every time you log in."

Cooked moves between Cringe and ClassClown, standing his ground. "That's enough, Cringe. We're here to play, not to deal with your nonsense. Why don't you find another room?"

Cringe tilts his head, feigning innocence. "Oh, I'm just getting started. You see, I like it here. And if you can't handle a little competition, maybe you should leave."

Suddenly, Glitch swings down, landing smoothly beside Cooked. "I think you've overstayed your welcome, Cringe," he says, his tone light but with a sharp edge. "We don't need your kind of drama."

Cringe's brow furrows, but he forces a laugh. "Oh, look, the silver monke is stepping in. You think you're gonna save them, Glitch? You're just as pathetic as they are."

Glitch's smile fades slightly. "I'm not here to save anyone. I'm here to make sure the game stays fun—for everyone. If you're not here for that, maybe it's you who doesn't belong."

The group watches the exchange in tense silence. It's clear that Cringe isn't backing down, but neither is Glitch. The bully's taunts have rattled them, but they're starting to find their resolve.

Griddy, her voice trembling but steady, steps forward.

"You know what, Cringe? I might not be the best at this game, but at least I'm having fun. That's what this is about, right?"

Cringe sneers, swinging away with a parting shot. "Yeah, keep telling yourself that. We'll see who's laughing when you're all tagged out."

He disappears into the shadows of the Forest, leaving the group shaken but standing together.

Cooked turns to the others, his eyes fixed with determination. "This isn't over. He's going to come back, and next time, we'll be ready."

Trekka nods, glancing towards Glitch. "And we've got an ally on our side now. We're not alone in this fight."

Glitch gives them a small, confident smile. "You've got more allies than you think. But we'll deal with Cringe together—when the time is right."

The Forest map is filled with the sound of rushing wind and the ruffle of leaves as the group swings into action, spreading out to prepare for Infection Mode. They can still feel the unease from their encounter with Cringe, but they push forward, determined not to let him ruin their game.

Tactix takes charge, his voice calm and steady. "Alright, everyone, listen up. We stick together. Use the double walls for height and keep moving. If we work as a team, we can outmaneuver him."

Swizzler nods, helping boost Griddy up onto a higher branch. "You've got this, Griddy! Just keep your grip loose and swing with confidence."

Griddy's face is set with determination. "I'm not letting him get to me. Not this time."

Just as the group starts to settle into a rhythm, Cringe reappears, swinging down from a high branch with a smug grin plastered across his face. "Look at you all, scurrying around like scared little monke's. Pathetic."

ClassClown rolls his eyes, still trying to keep things light. "Oh great, it's Cringe again. I thought I smelled something funny."

Cooked, not amused this time, steps forward. "We're done playing your game, Cringe. Either join us fairly or leave."

Cringe's laughter echoes through the trees, loud and mocking. "Join you? You're a joke. I'm here to show you all how real players dominate."

Without warning, he lunges forward, tagging Griddy in one swift motion. She stumbles back, stunned and upset. "Hey, I wasn't even ready!"

Cringe swings around her, taunting. "Of course you weren't. That's what makes it so easy."

Glitch, who's been watching quietly from a distance, finally steps in. He swings down smoothly, landing between Cringe and the rest of the group. "Enough, Cringe," Glitch says, his voice colder than they've ever heard it. "This isn't about skill for you—it's about making people feel small. But not today."

Cringe scoffs, but there's a flicker of uncertainty in his eyes. "Oh please, Glitch. Don't act like you're some kind of hero. You're just as much of a glitch in this game as I am."

Glitch thins his eyes, a dangerous smile tugging at his lips. "Maybe. But I know the difference between challenging players and bullying them. And so does the game."

Cooked catches on to what Glitch is implying and starts rallying the team. "You heard him, guys. We've trained for this. Use everything we've practiced. Double walls, branching, everything."

Tactix immediately directs the group. "Swizzler, take Griddy higher. ClassClown, keep him distracted with your jokes. Trekka, you scout the area—look for any advantage points."

Griddy, boosted by the team's support, pushes herself harder than ever before. She makes it up to the highest branch she's ever climbed. "I did it! I'm up here!" she shouts triumphantly.

Cringe snarls, swinging wildly towards her. "Not for long!" But before he can reach her, Swizzler swoops in, blocking his path with a perfect wall jump.

"Not today, Cringe," Swizzler says with a grin. "You're not tagging her again."

Cringe looks around, realizing the group has him surrounded. His bravado starts to crack. "What is this? Some kind of ambush?"

"It's called teamwork," Tactix replies sharply. "Something you clearly don't understand."

Glitch takes this moment to swing closer, his movements so fast they're almost a blur. "And you know what happens to players who abuse the game?"

Cringe's face twists in fear. "You wouldn't dare."

"Oh, I would," Glitch says with a smirk. He raises his arm, and a notification sound echoes through the Forest—REPORT SENT.

The group watches in stunned silence as Cringe's avatar glitches and begins to fade, his voice now panicked and full of rage. "This isn't fair! You can't do this to me!"

Cooked steps forward, arms crossed. "Fair? You never played fair, Cringe. Maybe it's time you learned what that feels like."

With one last flicker, Cringe disappears, leaving nothing but the sound of the wind rustling through the trees.

The group exhales collectively, the tension melting away. Griddy, still perched on her high branch, lets out a whoop of joy. "We did it! We actually stood up to him!"

ClassClown swings over, giving her a high-five. "And we did it with style!"

Glitch lands softly in front of them, offering a small, satisfied smile. "Nice work, team. You handled yourselves well."

Trekka steps closer, a curious look in her eyes. "You knew he was going to act like that, didn't you?"

Glitch shrugs. "Let's just say I've dealt with players like Cringe before. Bullies never last long when the game's real heroes step up."

Cooked gives him a fist bump, grinning. "Well, you're definitely one of us now."

Before they can celebrate further, the sound of footsteps echoes again—heavier, deliberate.

Tactix looks around, suddenly on edge. "We might have dealt with Cringe, but something tells me we've got another challenge coming."

Glitch tilts his head towards the deeper part of the Forest, a glint of excitement in his eyes. "Sounds like more game play. Who's ready for the next adventure?"

The Forest slowly settles into a tranquil silence after Cringe's abrupt exit. The sunlight filters through the branches, casting long, golden shadows as the day turns to dusk in the game. The group gathers together on the flat top of the central tree stump, catching their breath after the chaotic encounter.

Griddy swings over, beaming with pride. "I can't believe we actually handled that! I've never felt so... strong."

Swizzler grins, giving her a high five. "That's because you were strong, Griddy. You made it all the way up there today. You're leveling up faster than ever!"

ClassClown jumps in, feigning tears. "Look at us— going from noobs to pros in one day! I'm getting all emotional here."

The group laughs, the tension finally lifting. Tactix, ever the strategist, rubs his chin thoughtfully. "Jokes aside, that was intense. We dealt with Cringe well, but there's definitely something more going on here—especially with Glitch. He handled that situation like he knew it was coming."

Trekka nods, her mind still on the hidden tunnel. "And he seemed to know about the secret path too. It's like he's been planning this."

Cooked, always direct, turns to Glitch. "Alright, Glitch, spill it. You seem to know way more about this map and the players here than you're letting on."

Glitch just smirks, leaning back against the tree. "Let's just say I've been around the Forest long enough to know when things are about to get... interesting."

Griddy frowns, tilting her head. "Interesting how?"

Before Glitch can answer, a deep, rumbling noise echoes through the Forest. It's a sound they've never heard before, like the groan of something shifting underground.

Tactix's eyes go wide. "What was that? It sounded like it came from the direction of the secret tunnel."

Trekka's heart races. She remembers the tunnel from earlier, the one she spotted when Shadow disappeared. "I knew it! There's definitely something hidden down there."

Glitch stands up, his expression serious now. "You're right, Trekka. But you're not ready to explore it just yet. You've got more to learn before you dive into the unknown."

Cooked cracks a smile, clapping his hands together. "Courage? We've got plenty of that. But maybe we should save the heroics for tomorrow."

Swizzler nods in agreement. "Yeah, it's getting late, and we've been playing for hours. We should probably call it a night and meet up again tomorrow."

ClassClown stretches, yawning dramatically. "Good idea. Besides, I need a break—my arms are starting to feel like wet noodles!"

Griddy laughs, swinging to the ground. "Alright, same time tomorrow?"

Tactix nods, giving a thumbs up. "You know it. Let's log off and meet up tomorrow in ArmsUp. We've got a mystery to solve and more skills to practice."

As they each log out, Cooked stays behind for a moment, glancing at Glitch. "You'll be here tomorrow, right?"

Glitch gives a small, knowing smile. "I wouldn't miss it. Things are just starting to get good."

Cooked logs out with a grin, leaving the Forest empty once again. The last thing he hears is the sound of footsteps—soft, deliberate, and echoing through the quiet trees.

In the darkness of the empty Forest, Glitch's voice lingers softly in the wind, "Hope you're ready, team. Tomorrow is going to be wild."

4 GHOST IN THE GRAVEYARD

The crew logs back in the next night, eager to pick up where they left off. They gather at their usual spot, the flat top of the central tree stump, chatting excitedly about the crazy events of the previous game. The air is cool, and the sound of leaves whispering in the wind fills the Forest map. It's as if the entire world is holding its breath, waiting for what's about to happen next.

Cooked, always the one to get things started, claps his hands together. "Alright, team. Last night was wild, but tonight we're stepping it up a notch."

ClassClown chimes in with a grin, "Stepping it up? You mean like my impressive step-slip-and-fall move?"

The group laughs, their spirits high as they swing from branch to branch, warming up for whatever adventure awaits.

Suddenly, Glitch appears out of nowhere, landing gracefully beside them with a wide grin. "Hey, crew. I've got something different planned for tonight," he announces, his voice filled with excitement.

Trekka leans forward, intrigued. "Different? What do you have in mind, Glitch?"

Glitch's eyes light up with a mischievous gleam. "Ever heard of Ghost in the Graveyard?"

Swizzler raises an eyebrow. "A mini-game? I've heard some kids talking about it, but I've never played."

Tactix nods, rubbing his chin thoughtfully. "I've seen it mentioned, but I don't know the rules."

Glitch grins even wider, swinging up to a nearby branch. "Well, tonight's your lucky night. I guarantee it's going to be a blast—and maybe a bit spooky too."

Griddy's eyes widen with excitement. "Spooky? I love spooky games! What's it about?"

Glitch motions for them to gather closer. "It's simple," he says, lowering his voice like he's sharing a secret. "One of us will be the ghost—the tagger. They'll hide somewhere in the Forest while the rest of you search for them. When someone finds the ghost, they yell 'Ghost in the Graveyard!' and everyone has to run to the safe spot—the treehouse."

Cooked looks intrigued. "And if the ghost tags you before you get there?"

"Then you join the ghost's team," Glitch explains. "It gets crazier each round as more players become ghosts. By the end, it's a full-on chase to the treehouse."

ClassClown can't resist a joke. "So basically, it's like every one of my games—me running away and screaming for my life."

The group laughs, the excitement bubbling up as they imagine the chaos of the game.

"Are you guys ready to play?" Glitch asks, hopping down with a challenging grin.

Trekka punches the air, pumped up. "Absolutely! This sounds awesome."

Cooked nods in agreement. "Let's do it. Who's going to be the first ghost?"

Glitch's smile turns sly. "I'll go first. Let's see if you

can keep up."

The crew exchanges determined glances, their adrenaline kicking in. Little do they know, this game is about to bring more than just fun—it's going to reveal hidden skills, new strategies, and a test of their teamwork like never before.

The group gathers in a circle, standing on the wide flat top of the central tree stump. The excitement in the air is palpable as they lean in, eager to hear more about the mini-game. Glitch takes the lead, pacing around like a coach giving a pep talk.

"Alright, listen up," Glitch says, clapping his hands together for emphasis. "This game is called Ghost in the Graveyard, and it's all about stealth, speed, and strategy."

ClassClown raises his hand with exaggerated seriousness. "Quick question—does screaming and flailing count as a strategy? Because if so, I'm going pro."

The group bursts into laughter, and Glitch shakes his head, chuckling. "Actually, it might help you run faster, so sure, let's call it a strategy."

Tactix, always focused on the details, steps forward. "So, you said one player starts as the ghost. What's the best way to avoid getting tagged?"

Glitch grins, clearly enjoying the attention. "Good question, Tactix. The key is staying unpredictable. Don't just run in a straight line or hide in the obvious spots. Keep your movement random and stay alert."

Griddy's eyes are wide with excitement. "And then we all run to the treehouse, right? That's the safe spot?"

"Exactly," Glitch confirms. "But here's the twist—the ghost can tag anyone who doesn't make it to the treehouse in time. If you get tagged, you join the ghost's team for the next round."

Trekka leans against a branch, thinking it over. "So, it's like Infection Mode but with a twist. The ghost's team gets bigger and bigger until there's only one player left."

Glitch nods, giving her an approving smile. "You got it, Trekka. And that's when the real challenge begins. The last player standing has to dodge all the ghosts to make it to the treehouse. It's fast, it's chaotic, and it's a total adrenaline rush."

Swizzler grins, bouncing on his fists. "I'm ready. This sounds awesome. Any tips for us, Glitch?"

Glitch pauses, pretending to think. "Hmm, let's see. If you're searching for the ghost, spread out and use branching to cover more ground. If you're the last one standing, don't be afraid to take risks—sometimes the best move is the unexpected one."

Cooked cracks his knuckles, looking determined. "Alright, we've got the rules. Let's do this. Who's going to be the ghost?"

Glitch's eyes gleam with mischief as he raises his hand. "I'll go first. But I warn you, I'm not going to make it easy."

ClassClown lets out a playful groan. "Oh great, we're going up against the expert ghost first. This is going to be Sigma!"

Tactix claps his hands together, rallying the group. "Alright, team—let's spread out and keep our eyes open. And remember, don't panic when you hear the call. Just run for the treehouse."

Griddy pumps her fist in the air. "Let's do this! I've never been more ready."

Glitch nods, stepping back into the shadows. "Alright then, count to ten and let the hunt begin."

As the group closes their eyes and starts counting, the atmosphere shifts, the playful banter replaced with a tension that makes the hairs on the back of their necks stand up. Somewhere in the darkened forest, Glitch is already hiding, ready to scare the life out of them.

The group finishes counting down, their voices echoing through the forest. "Ten... nine... eight..."

With the final number, they spring into action, splitting up to search the map. The playful mood is replaced by focused determination. The only sound is fists thumping as they move through the trees.

Tactix gestures towards the double walls. "I'll take the high route—keep an eye on the branches below."

Swizzler swings from branch to branch, scanning the shadows. "He's got to be hiding somewhere tricky. Check the corners of the map and behind the big rocks."

ClassClown, trying his best to be stealthy, trips over a root and lands flat on his back. "I'm definitely blending in," he mutters, peeking out from behind a small bush. "Nobody will spot me here."

Griddy stifles a laugh. "ClassClown, you're about as hidden as a banana in a monkey's hand."

Trekka, exploring near the right side of the map, pauses as she hears a faint shuffling sound coming from the bushes. Her heart races as she signals for the others to join her quietly.

"I think I found something," she whispers, her eyes darting towards the noise.

The group gathers around, inching closer. The tension builds as they creep forward, barely breathing. Then, without warning, Trekka leaps back and shouts, "Ghost in the Graveyard!"

The forest erupts into chaos. Everyone scrambles in different directions, racing towards the treehouse—the designated safe spot.

"Run!" Cooked yells, leading the charge. "Head for the treehouse, now!"

Swizzler swings ahead, showing off his speed. "Last ones to the treehouse is getting tagged!"

Behind them, Glitch bolts from his hiding spot, the

ghost revealed. He moves with incredible speed, closing in on ClassClown, who's lagging behind.

"I knew I should have skipped leg day—oh wait, we don't have legs!" ClassClown jokes, flinging himself onto a lower branch in a desperate attempt to escape.

Trekka makes it to the treehouse first, turning to help pull Griddy up the last few feet. "Hurry, Griddy! He's right behind you!"

With a final burst of effort, Griddy reaches the platform just as Glitch lunges, tagging Swizzler instead. "Gotcha!" Glitch says with a grin. "You almost made it."

Swizzler laughs, catching his breath. "Okay, I'm officially on the ghost team now. Who's next?"

Cooked gives a playful salute. "Alright, crew—we've got our work cut out for us. Let's see who's really got the moves."

The game isn't over yet, and as they regroup for the next round, the adrenaline is pumping. Somewhere deeper in the forest, the distant echo of footsteps hints that they might not be the only ones playing tonight.

The crew huddles together in the treehouse, their laughter and shouts echoing through the Forest. Griddy peeks over the edge, trying to spot any movement below. Swizzler, now part of the ghost crew after being tagged earlier, disappears into the shadows with Glitch, ready to hide.

"Are you ready yet?" ClassClown yells, cupping his hands around his mouth.

A few moments of silence pass before Tactix joins in, tapping his fist impatiently. "Come on, ghosts! We're getting bored up here. Or are you too scared to play?"

Cooked, leaning back against the wall of the treehouse, grins at his friends. "They're probably taking their sweet time to make sure we don't find them. It's all part of their plan."

"Or maybe they're setting up the ultimate jump scare," Trekka adds, glancing nervously into the darkened forest.

Finally, a voice calls out from below, echoing through the trees. It's Glitch's playful tone. "We're ready! Come find us!"

The crew springs into action, leaping down from the treehouse in a flurry of movement. They spread out, eyes scanning the shadows as they search for the hidden ghosts.

Trekka sticks close to the edge of the Forest, her keen eyes spotting any flicker of movement. "Let's stay low and quiet," she whispers to Tactix. "We'll have a better chance of spotting them first."

Suddenly, Trekka yells, "Ghost in the Graveyard!" Her voice is filled with excitement as she bolts back to the treehouse for safety, juking and dodging to avoid being tagged. She makes it—she's safe!

The others whip around, hearts pounding, and see Swizzler darting out from his hiding spot, lunging towards them with surprising speed. The crew scrambles, shouts and laughter filling the air as they race back towards the safety of the treehouse.

"Move, move, move!" Cooked shouts, leaping onto a branch and swinging up with a burst of speed. ClassClown slips, falling right into the tagger. "I'm too young to be a ghost!" he cries, as his monke color changes to red, signaling he's been tagged.

Griddy barely makes it to the base of the treehouse, fumbling up the stairs before Swizzler lunges at her. "Gotcha!" Swizzler shouts triumphantly. "You're too slow for the Tag Master!"

But the game isn't over yet. Cooked and Tactix are still out there, the last ones left untagged. Tactix darts between the trees, his breath coming in short gasps as he hears footsteps closing in behind him. It's all about survival now—he's too rushed to strategize as he finds himself surrounded by both Swizzler and Glitch.

Tactix fights back, ducking and weaving, but Glitch tags him with a swift move. "Gotcha, strategist," Glitch teases.

"Cooked, get to the treehouse!" Tactix shouts, his voice urgent. "You're the only one left!"

Cooked doesn't respond; he's too focused on staying ahead of the ghosts. He leaps onto a high branch, gripping it tightly as he swings himself up. Below him, Glitch and Swizzler scan the area with sharp eyes.

"There he is!" Glitch yells, pointing up at Cooked's hiding spot.

In a split second, Cooked launches himself from the branch, barely avoiding their grasp. He's fast—faster than they expected—but the ghosts are right behind him, closing the gap as he tries to wall climb away.

Trekka watches from the treehouse, cheering him on. "You've got this, Cooked! Just a little further!" she shouts, fists clenched in excitement.

Cooked's arms pump as he sprints towards the treehouse roof. But just as he makes his final leap, Glitch lunges from the side with a swift, unexpected move. "You're cooked!" Glitch shouts as he tags him.

Now it's Trekka's turn. She's the only one left, the last survivor. The ghosts regroup, hiding in the shadows once more. "Are you ready yet?" Trekka yells from the treehouse, trying to sound braver than she feels.

From somewhere deep in the Forest, Glitch's voice calls back. "Ready whenever you are, Trekka."

She takes a deep breath and jumps down, her heart pounding. She knows they're out there, waiting. The suspense is thick as she creeps through the trees, scanning every shadow. Suddenly, she spots them—

Glitch, Swizzler, and the rest of the ghost crew, lurking in a circle around her.

Before she can react, they all pounce at once, tagging her from every side. Her piercing scream echoes through the Forest, a mix of surprise and laughter. "You got me!" she gasps, collapsing to the ground in a fit of giggles.

The group gathers at the picnic table, exhausted but exhilarated, sharing their stories of close calls and classic fails. As they settle down, the distant echo of heavy footsteps reaches their ears once again, louder and closer this time.

Cooked exchanges a worried glance with Glitch. "We're not alone out here, are we?"

Glitch shakes his head slowly, his usual grin replaced with a serious expression. "Nope. And whoever it is, they're not playing around."

The crew's laughter slowly fading as they catch their breath from the intense game of Ghost in the Graveyard. Trekka's face is flushed with excitement, and even ClassClown, who had been tagged early, can't stop grinning.

"That was epic!" Cooked exclaims, wiping sweat from his brow. "I didn't think I'd get tagged like that, Glitch. You've got some serious moves."

Glitch chuckles, his usual playful smirk back on his face. "You guys aren't half bad yourselves. It's been a while since I've had this much fun."

Swizzler nods, giving Griddy a high-five. "We've got to do this again. Same time tomorrow?"

Tactix, ever the strategist, looks thoughtful. "Yeah, I'm in. But there's something that's been bugging me," he says, glancing over at Glitch. "How did you find our private room anyway? And what about Shadow, Cringe? They knew how to get in too."

The group goes quiet, exchanging uneasy glances. It's

the first time they've really thought about it, and the realization sends a shiver down their spines.

Griddy, her cheerful expression faltering, asks, "You didn't share the code, did you, ClassClown?"

ClassClown holds up his hands defensively. "What? Me? No way! I'd never sell out our secret room—unless there was a lot of shiny rocks involved," he jokes, but there's a nervous edge to his laughter.

Cooked's smile fades as he looks at Glitch. "So, how did you get in here? We're pretty careful about who we share the code with."

Glitch tilts his head, giving them a look that's hard to read. "I have my ways," he says cryptically. "Let's just say I'm good at finding things—and people. But if it makes you feel better, I'm here to play, not to mess with your group."

Trekka narrows her eyes slightly, sensing there's more to the story. "Still, it's strange. It's almost like someone's leaking our private room info."

The tension in the air thickens, and for a moment, the fun and lighthearted atmosphere from earlier is gone. The crew exchanges wary looks, each one wondering if there's a mole among them.

Glitch stands up and stretches, breaking the silence. "Well, this has been great, but I think it's time we all log off. Rest up—you're gonna need it for tomorrow."

Cooked nods slowly, his eyes widening. "Yeah, tomorrow night, same time. Let's meet up and settle this once and for all."

"Agreed," Tactix says, giving a firm nod. "We'll figure this out together."

As they all prepare to log off, Trekka gives one last look around the Forest, feeling a chill she can't quite explain. "See you all tomorrow," she says with a forced smile.

Glitch waves, his grin wide and mysterious. "Oh, I wouldn't miss it for the world."

With that, they each log out one by one, their avatars disappearing into thin air. But the echo of heavy footsteps lingers in the empty Forest long after they're gone, as if someone—or something—is still watching.

Cooked, always thinking one step ahead, hides in the control room after his friends log out, his heart pounding in his chest. He checks the player count, expecting it to drop—but it doesn't. There are still three players in the private room, including himself. In the real world, Cooked pulls off his VR headset, his mind racing. This isn't just a game among friends anymore, and he knows they're not alone.

5 MYSTERY IN THE BEACH CAVE

The crew logs back into their private room, ArmsUp, energized from last night's epic game of Ghost in the Graveyard. The sun dips lower in the Forest map, casting long, eerie shadows through the dense canopy. It's the perfect setting for another thrilling night, but there's an unease hanging in the air that wasn't there before.

Cooked, swinging up to the central tree stump, gathers the group. "Alright, everyone," he begins, his orange monke leaning forward with a serious expression. "Before we get started, I need to tell you something strange."

"What's up?" Swizzler asks, already hanging from a branch with his usual agility.

Cooked glances around, making sure they're all listening. "Last night, after you all logged off, I stayed behind for a bit," he says quietly. "Just to check something."

Tactix raises an eyebrow. "Check what?"

"The player count," Cooked replies. "When you all left, there were still three players logged in, including me."

A hush falls over the group as the realization sinks in. "Wait… that means there were two other players still in the room?" Griddy asks, her purple monke fidgeting nervously.

"Exactly," Cooked nods. "And I didn't see anyone else. Whoever it was, they were hiding."

Trekka's eyes grow sus, and she instinctively looks towards the Beach Cave, shrouded in darkness at the edge of the map. "It has to be someone skilled enough to avoid us, even when we were searching," she says.

ClassClown tries to break the tension with a joke, but his voice wavers. "Maybe it's just a couple of ghosts who forgot to log out," he chuckles nervously. "Or maybe… we've got some stalkers."

Tactix's face grows serious. "This isn't random," he says firmly. "Someone knew our private room code."

"Shadow," Swizzler says quietly, his tone darkening. "It has to be him. And maybe he's not alone."

As if on cue, a faint sound drifts out from the direction of the Beach Cave—mocking laughter, followed by the unmistakable click of a camera shutter.

"Did you guys hear that?" Griddy whispers, inching closer to the group.

Cooked's expression hardens. "We're not alone," he says. "And I think it's time we find out who's been spying on us."

The crew starts making their way towards the Beach Cave, tension building with every step. Somewhere in the darkness, two shadows move deeper into the cave, waiting for the perfect moment to strike.

The crew edges closer to the Beach Cave, their senses on high alert. The light fades quickly here, leaving only the soft glow of moonlight reflecting off the rippling water. The cave entrance yawns before them, dark and foreboding, like a mouth ready to swallow them whole.

"Stay close," Tactix whispers, leading the way. "Whatever's in there, we need to face it together."

Cooked nods in agreement, his expression steely. "Whoever it is, they've been hiding for too long. Let's flush them out."

ClassClown, attempting to lighten the mood, quips, "Well, if it's a troll, I'm ready with my best anti-troll jokes. Just hope they have a sense of humor."

But as they move deeper into the cave, the laughter fades, replaced by the sound of hushed voices echoing off the stone walls. Cooked signals for everyone to stop, and they huddle together, listening.

"Get the camera ready," a voice says, loud enough for them to hear now. It's smug, dripping with condescension. "This is going to be gold. These noobs have no idea they've been our content farm."

Another voice chuckles, a familiar, sinister laugh. "Keep rolling, Trollz. The fans are going to eat this up."

Griddy's eyes widen as she recognizes the second voice. "It's Shadow," she whispers, fear threading through her words.

"And who's Trollz?" Swizzler asks, peering into the darkness.

Before anyone can answer, a flash of light blinds them momentarily. The crew stumbles back, shielding their eyes as the source of the light steps into view—an obnoxious neon green monke, holding a virtual camera and wearing a vexing grin.

"Ladies and gentlemen, the show has arrived!" Trollz announces, flourishing his arms like a circus ringmaster. "And you've all been the unwitting stars of my latest video."

Shadow emerges from the shadows behind him, his black monke avatar almost blending into the darkness of the cave. "Say cheese," he sneers. "You're about to go viral for all the wrong reasons."

Tactix steps forward, fists clenched. "You've been spying on us this whole time? Recording us without our knowledge?"

Trollz doesn't even flinch. Instead, he swings the camera towards Tactix's face, zooming in. "Oh, come on, don't act so surprised," he taunts. "Shadow and I have been planning this for weeks. We've got hours of footage of your embarrassing fails and noob moves. The fans are going to love it."

Cooked's face turns red with anger. "You think this is funny? You've invaded our private room, and now you want to humiliate us online?"

"Bingo," Trollz says with a grin, spinning the camera back around to his own face for a close-up. "But don't worry—you'll all be famous by tomorrow. You can thank me later."

ClassClown, despite the tension, manages a forced laugh. "Famous? More like infamous. But hey, I always wanted to be a meme."

Trekka, her face a mask of fury, steps up next to Cooked. "This isn't a joke, Trollz. You've crossed a line."

Trollz just shrugs. "Lines are meant to be crossed," he says coolly. "Now, smile for the camera. This is your big moment."

The camera's red recording light blinks ominously in the darkness, reflecting in the crew's eyes. Cooked takes a deep breath, steeling himself. "This isn't over, Trollz," he says quietly. "Not by a long shot."

The crew takes off in a frenzy, sprinting out of the Beach Cave and back toward the Forest map, their safe haven. The familiar sight of the towering trees and dense branches offers a small comfort, but the heavy feeling of betrayal lingers in the air. They leap across the big rock connecting the maps, not daring to look back. The echoes of Trollz's laughter follow them like a dark shadow, mingling with the sound of rustling leaves.

As they regroup at the base of the central tree, everyone's breathing hard, adrenaline pumping. Cooked spins around, looking at his friends. "We need to talk," he says, his voice firm. "Something's been off, and I think it's time we clear the air."

Tactix nods, his face clouded with suspicion. "Yeah, I've been thinking the same thing. How did Trollz and Shadow get into our private room in the first place?"

A silence falls over the group, everyone exchanging uncertain glances. Griddy looks down, pounding at the dirt. "We set the room to private, right? No one else should have the code."

ClassClown shifts uncomfortably, avoiding eye contact. His usual joking demeanor is gone, replaced by a nervous tension. "Maybe… maybe they guessed it?" he mumbles, but it's clear he doesn't believe his own words.

Trekka's eyes grows firm as she steps closer to him. "ClassClown, are you sure? Because I've got a feeling you know more than you're letting on."

Cooked's expression softens, but there's a hard edge to his voice. "If you know something, you need to tell us now. We're a team, remember?"

ClassClown's shoulders slump, and he finally looks up, his eyes filled with guilt. "Alright, fine," he admits, his voice small. "I… I gave them the code."

The words hang in the air like a slap to the face. Everyone freezes, processing what they've just heard. Tactix clenches his fists, taking a step back. "You what?"

Swizzler's face twists in disbelief. "Dude, why would you do that? You know how much this room means to us."

ClassClown swallows hard, the shame evident on his face. "They threatened me, okay?" he blurts out.

"Shadow and Trollz, they've been bullying me at school for months. They said if I gave them the code, they'd leave me alone. I thought… I thought it was the only way to get them off my back."

Griddy steps forward, her expression softening with sympathy. "You should've told us, ClassClown. We would've helped you. You didn't have to do this alone."

Trekka sighs, her anger melting away. "We're your friends, no matter what. We would've stood up for you."

Cooked takes a deep breath, running a hand through his fur. "We get it, ClassClown," he says finally. "But you need to understand—you broke our trust. It's going to take time to earn that back."

ClassClown nods, tears welling up in his eyes. "I know, and I'm sorry. I really am. I didn't mean for it to get this far."

Just then, a familiar, mocking voice echoes through the trees. "Aw, look at this heartwarming moment," Trollz sneers, stepping into view with Shadow beside him. "So touching, I might cry."

The crew whirls around, instincts kicking in as they form a tight circle. Cooked glares at the two intruders. "You've had your fun, Trollz. But you're not welcome here. Get out."

Shadow smirks, cracking his knuckles. "Or what? You'll log off and cry about it?"

Tactix steps forward, his voice cold and calm. "No, we're not running anymore. This is our room, our game. And we're taking it back."

Trollz steps forward, holding his camera up, a smug grin plastered across his face. "This is even better than I hoped," he says, his eyes gleaming with delight. "A secret betrayal, a tearful confession—all caught on tape. This is going to get so many views."

ClassClown's face drains of color as he realizes what's

happening. "Wait… you've been recording this whole time?" he asks, his voice barely a whisper.

Trollz winks, his finger hovering over the camera lens. "Oh yeah, buddy. Every single word. I've got it all—your little sob story, the big friendship speech, all that drama. It's pure gold."

The crew exchanges shocked looks, the weight of the betrayal sinking in even deeper. Cooked's fists clench at his sides, his eyes blazing with anger. "You really don't know when to quit, do you, Trollz?"

Tactix steps closer, his voice low and dangerous. "Turn it off, Trollz. This isn't a joke anymore."

Trollz laughs, the sound echoing through the forest like a taunt. "Why would I turn it off now? The drama's just getting started. Besides, my viewers love a good meltdown."

Swizzler shakes his head, a mix of disbelief and fury on his face. "You're not going to get away with this."

Trollz smirks, holding the camera steady. "Oh, I think I already have. You're all just a bunch of noobs who fell right into my trap. Now smile for the camera—it's time to show the world who the real clowns are."

Trollz tilts his head, a sinister smile playing on his lips. "I hope you're ready for your fifteen minutes of fame," he says, still recording. "Because once this goes live, everyone's going to know exactly who you are."

The tension in the air is palpable, like the calm before a storm. The crew stands together, forming a tight circle at the base of the towering central tree. Cooked looks each of his friends in the eye, his expression serious. "We're not running anymore," he says firmly. "If they want a fight, we're giving them one."

Tactix nods in agreement, his analytical mind already piecing together a plan. "We need to use everything we've learned. This is our map, our home turf—we know it better than anyone."

Griddy clenches her fists, her usual bright smile replaced with a look of determination. "No more hiding. It's time we stand up for ourselves."

Trekka scans the tree line, her senses on high alert. "Shadow and Trollz are still out there, watching us. They've got something planned, but we'll be ready."

ClassClown steps forward, his voice cracking with guilt. "I'm so sorry, everyone. I never should have trusted them. I just wanted them to leave me alone at school."

Cooked places a hand on ClassClown's shoulder, giving him a reassuring nod. "We all make mistakes, but we're a team. We've got your back."

In the distance, the faint sound of mocking laughter drifts through the forest. It's Trollz, and he's still recording, taunting them from the shadows. "Oh, this is going to be good," his voice echoes. "I can't wait to see how you handle what's coming next."

The crew tightens their formation, adrenaline surging through their veins. They know the real battle hasn't even begun yet.

Cooked takes a deep breath, staring into the darkness. "Alright, team. This ends tonight. No more games—let's show them what we're made of."

As the group charges deeper into the forest, the sun casts long, eerie shadows behind them, setting the stage for the ultimate showdown that's about to unfold.

6 THE ULTIMATE SHOWDOWN

The air feels charged, like the moment before a storm breaks. The crew stands together in the middle of the Forest map, their usual playful banter replaced by a tense, focused silence. Shadows stretch long and dark, weaving between the towering trees as the sun begins to set in the virtual sky. The familiar sounds of birds chirping and leaves rustling are there, but now they seem different— like the forest is waiting, caught in a tense, uneasy silence.

Cooked steps forward, looking at his friends with grit. "We're not just playing tag anymore," he says, his voice low but steady. "Trollz and Shadow want a show? We'll give them a show they won't forget."

Swizzler cracks his knuckles, trying to mask the nervous energy with a confident grin. "Let's make sure they regret ever crashing our room."

Tactix nods, already forming strategies in his head. "We need to be smart about this. They'll try to split us up like before, make us panic. Stick together as much as you can, watch each other's backs, and don't let them get inside your head."

Griddy looks around, her eyes wide but filled with a

new sense of tenacity. "This time, we're ready for them," she says, clenching her fists. "We've practiced, we've learned, and we've got something they don't—each other."

ClassClown, for once, isn't cracking jokes. He steps closer to the group, guilt still hanging heavy in his expression. "I'm sorry, guys," he says quietly. "I messed up, but I'm here now. I want to help make this right."

Trekka places a reassuring hand on his shoulder. "We know, ClassClown. Let's focus on what's ahead. It's time to show them what our crew is really about."

Suddenly, a sound pierces the tense silence—a slow, mocking clap echoes through the forest, bouncing off the trees. The crew turns as one, their eyes locking onto the figures emerging from the shadows.

Trollz steps into view first, his face lit up by the glow of his camera, still recording every second. "Touching speech," he sneers. "Really got me right here." He taps his chest, feigning a look of sentiment before breaking into a mocking laugh.

Behind him, Shadow appears like a wraith, blending into the dark of the Forest with his sleek black form. He doesn't say a word, but the smirk on his face says it all—he's ready to play, and he's ready to win.

Cooked takes a deep breath, then steps forward to face them. "Alright, team," he says, his voice steady but laced with resolve. "This ends tonight. No more games—let's show them what we're made of."

The forest falls silent, the air dense with anticipation. The showdown they've been building towards is finally here, and there's no turning back.

The crew moves silently through the Forest, their faces set with willpower. Tonight isn't about practice or friendly competition. It's a showdown, a test of everything they've learned and a chance to prove they're stronger together. Cooked leads the way, his eyes scanning the branches above for any sign of movement.

"We need a plan," Tactix says, his voice hushed but urgent. "Trollz and Shadow are out for blood, and they'll use every dirty trick in the book."

"Agreed," Cooked replies, turning to the group. "We split up, but stay close enough to regroup if needed. Trekka, keep an eye on the secret tunnel—we can't let them ambush us from behind. Swizzler, you and Griddy stick together. Use the double walls for quick escapes."

Griddy nods, her usual nervousness replaced by a steely resolve. "I've got this," she says, glancing at Swizzler, who gives her a reassuring nod.

ClassClown, trying to lighten the mood, chimes in, "I'll be the distraction, obviously. I've got jokes they've never heard before—this time, I'm going all out."

"Just don't get tagged too quickly, okay?" Trekka teases, but there's an edge to her voice. They all know what's at stake tonight.

Suddenly, a dark shape darts between the trees, and the crew falls silent. It's Shadow, his black monke coat blending seamlessly into the shadows. He stops, just a flash of a grin visible in the moonlight before he vanishes into the treetops.

"He's taunting us," Swizzler mutters. "They want us to chase them."

"We can't fall for it," Tactix says sharply. "It's a trap. They're trying to split us up."

Cooked clenches his fists. "Then we flip the script. We don't play their game—we make them play ours. Tactix, lead us through the lower branches. Keep us hidden until we're ready to strike."

The crew takes off, moving like a single unit. They leap from branch to branch, using every skill they've practiced. Griddy, who once struggled with even the simplest jumps, now navigates the double walls with surprising speed.

Tactix pauses, looking back at Cooked. "On your signal."

Cooked nods, watching the treetops for any sign of their opponents. Then he spots them—Trollz and Shadow, perched high above, watching the crew with predatory eyes. Trollz holds up his camera, still recording, a smug smile on his face.

"Now!" Cooked shouts.

In a blur of movement, the crew launches their attack. Swizzler swings wide, circling around to flank them. Trekka dives towards the secret tunnel, blocking it off to prevent an escape. Tactix guides Griddy up a series of branches, setting her up for a surprise tag from above.

The forest erupts in chaos as the battle begins.

The forest is a blur of movement as the crew charges toward their opponents. Cooked leads the assault, directing the team with precision. "Swizzler, keep flanking! Trekka, hold the tunnel!" The air is heavy with tension, but there's a shift—an unspoken understanding between the friends. They've got each other's backs, and this time, they're ready.

Up in the branches, ClassClown watches the chaos unfold below. He spots Trollz, still holding his camera, zooming in on each member of the crew as they struggle. The taunting voice of Trollz rings out, "Look at these noobs—they don't stand a chance!"

A flicker of fortitude crosses ClassClown's face. He's had enough of the insults, the belittling, and the feeling of helplessness. He takes a deep breath and swings down from his perch, landing directly in front of Trollz and Shadow.

"Well, well, if it isn't the comedian," Trollz sneers, lowering his camera slightly. "You finally decided to show up for the real game?"

ClassClown straightens up, the usual playful spark back in his eyes. "Oh, I'm here alright," he says, grinning. "But you know what, Trollz? You've got the punchline all wrong."

Shadow moves closer, eyes confused. "What are you talking about?"

ClassClown glances back at his crew, then looks Trollz dead in the eye. "The joke's on you," he says loudly, his voice ringing with newfound confidence. "Because while you've been busy recording us, we've been setting you up for the perfect trap."

He winks at Tactix, who catches on immediately. "Now, ClassClown!" Tactix shouts, signaling the rest of the crew.

With a sudden burst of speed, ClassClown lunges forward, juking left then right, using every trick he's learned from his friends. He bounces off the nearest tree, his movements unpredictable and fluid. Trollz, caught off guard, fumbles with his camera, trying to keep up.

"What's going on?" Trollz shouts, stumbling back as ClassClown closes the distance.

"Just a little lesson in humor," ClassClown replies, laughing. "You see, the best jokes are the ones that surprise you."

Before Trollz can react, ClassClown tags him, his hand slapping down on Trollz's shoulder with a satisfying thump. "Gotcha!" he exclaims triumphantly.

The crew erupts in cheers. Swizzler whoops from the sidelines, and Trekka pumps her fist in the air. "That was awesome!" she yells.

Shadow looks stunned, his usual smirk wiped clean off his face. "How...?" he starts, but ClassClown cuts him off.

"You underestimated me," ClassClown says, his voice

calm but powerful. "You thought I was just here for the jokes. But it turns out, I'm a lot better at this game than you thought."

Griddy swings down from a high branch, landing beside ClassClown. "That was incredible!" she says, clapping him on the back. "You completely fooled them."

ClassClown flashes his friends a genuine smile, the weight of his guilt lifting. "I just remembered what you all taught me," he says. "Teamwork makes the dream work, right?"

Cooked steps forward, offering ClassClown a fist bump. "You nailed it, buddy. We couldn't have done this without you."

ClassClown bumps fists with Cooked, then turns to Trollz and Shadow, who are both still recovering from the shock. "Oh, and Trollz," ClassClown says, leaning in close. "You might want to delete that footage. It doesn't look good when the pranksters end up being the punchline."

Trollz, still recording, forces a smile, but there's a crack in his confidence. "This isn't over," he mutters, but his voice wavers. For the first time, it's clear that the crew has turned the tables.

With Trollz tagged, the tide has turned. The crew forms a tight circle around Shadow, who stands with his back against the central tree. He looks cornered, his eyes flicking from one friend to the next, searching for a way out.

Cooked steps forward, his hand extended in a rare gesture of camaraderie. "It's over, Shadow. You've lost. You don't have to play like this anymore. Join us—for real this time."

The forest seems to hold its tension as the offer hangs in the air. Shadow's face contorts, the anger melting away, replaced by something softer—almost regretful. He looks at Cooked's outstretched hand, then back at the crew, who watch him with hope, their earlier frustration now replaced with a sense of cautious optimism.

For a moment, it feels like they've reached him. The tense standoff softens, and Shadow takes a step forward. "You really think I'd want to join your little crew?" he ~~asks~~ sneers.

Tactix nods, his voice gentle. "You don't have to be the villain, Shadow. You can be part of something better."

Shadow's lips curl into a smile, but it's not a warm one. It's cold, calculating. He tilts his head, as if considering the offer, then chuckles darkly. "Oh, you naive fools," he says, shaking his head. "You actually believe this is over? You've seen nothing yet."

Trekka takes a step back, her face falling. "What are you talking about, Shadow?"

Shadow's grin widens, his eyes gleaming with a sinister glint. "You think tagging me ends the game? I've already got plans in motion—plans you won't see coming. This is just the beginning."

Before anyone can respond, Trollz, who had been sitting off to the side, suddenly jumps forward, a smug grin plastered across his face. He raises his headset slightly, his thumb hovering over the power button. "Oh, and by the way," Trollz says, giving them all a mocking salute, "this whole heartfelt moment? It's all on tape. Let's see how your little redemption story plays out when it's live-streamed for everyone to laugh at."

Cooked's eyes widen, and he lunges forward. "No, ~~wait—~~"

But it's too late. With a synchronized, almost theatrical move, both Trollz and Shadow power off their headsets. Their avatars disappear, leaving the crew standing there, stunned and speechless.

The silence that follows is deafening. It's as if the entire Forest map has been drained of sound, the usual rustle of leaves and chirping birds eerily absent.

Griddy breaks the silence, her voice barely a whisper. "What just happened?"

"They're gone," Tactix mutters, staring at the empty space where Shadow and Trollz had been. "But something tells me this isn't the last we've seen of them."

Cooked clenches his fists, his jaw set with conviction. "They may have run this time," he says quietly, "but we'll be ready for them next time. This isn't over."

The crew gathers together, their earlier victory now overshadowed by a looming sense of dread. Trekka glances at Cooked, her eyes filled with worry. "Do you really think they'll be back?"

Cooked looks out into the darkened Forest, the shadows seeming deeper and more menacing than before. "Oh, they'll be back," he says, his voice low and resolute. "And next time, we won't just be playing to win—we'll be playing to end this for good."

7 BIRTHDAY BASH

The crew logs in one by one, gathering at the familiar flat top of the central tree stump in the Forest map. This time, though, they're not just here to play—they've got a plan.

"Alright, everyone," Cooked says, his tone serious but with a playful spark in his eye. "Before we do anything else, let's change the room code."

Tactix nods in agreement. "We need something new, something they can't guess."

"How about 'School'?" Griddy suggests. "It's where we all met, and it shows we're ready to learn from everything that happened."

The crew exchanges approving nods, and they all type in the new code: School. The room resets, and a sense of relief washes over them, like they've closed the door on the chaos caused by Trollz and Shadow.

Just as they settle into the new room, Swizzler logs in. He barely has time to adjust his headset when the entire crew erupts into a coordinated shout: "Happy Birthday, Swizzler!"

Bright virtual balloons fill the screen, popping up all

around him. The crew starts dancing, their avatars bouncing in a celebratory circle.

Swizzler stands there, stunned. His usual cool demeanor melts away, replaced by a huge, genuine smile. "No way! You guys did all this for me?" he asks, his voice cracking with surprise.

Trekka steps forward, grinning ear to ear. "Of course we did! We couldn't let your birthday pass without a party—especially after everything we've been through. You deserve a celebration, Swizzler."

Swizzler looks around at his friends, visibly moved. "I thought we were just logging in for practice today. This is... amazing. Thank you."

Griddy bounces up and down with excitement. "And that's not all! Wait till you see what we've got planned next—we're taking you shopping at City!"

The crew exchanges eager glances, ready to show Swizzler the surprise they've been planning. "You're going to love it," Cooked says with a wink. "We've got a whole adventure lined up for your special day."

The crew bounds excitedly into the City mall, the vibrant hub of cosmetics and accessories. They spread out, running from shop to shop, with Swizzler at the center of the action.

"We've got a surprise for you, birthday boy!" Cooked grins, loading a small bundle of shiny rocks into Swizzler's account. "This one's on us. Pick whatever you want—it's your day."

Swizzler's eyes widen. "Seriously? You guys didn't have to do this!"

Tactix gives a nod, his expression softening. "Of course we did. We stick together, remember? Now go get yourself some new drip."

Swizzler darts into the cosmetics shop, his avatar practically vibrating with excitement. He tries on a giant party hat first, followed by a pair of oversized nerd glasses. The crew bursts into laughter as ClassClown mimics him, striking a silly pose.

"How about this?" Swizzler says, selecting a flashy pair of neon sunglasses and a bright, floating party balloon.

"Perfect choice," Trekka says with a smile. "You look like you're ready to start the party."

Back in the Forest map, Griddy flips on her microphone and starts playing an upbeat playlist. Music fills the air, echoing through the trees and adding an electric vibe to the celebration. "Alright, who's ready for a dance-off?" she shouts.

The crew scrambles to the roof above the picnic table, daring each other to show their best moves without falling off. Cooked kicks things off with uncontrollable spins. ClassClown, not to be outdone, flails his arms wildly, doing the most exaggerated dance moves anyone's ever seen.

"Is that a dance or an emergency signal?" Tactix jokes, barely able to keep a straight face.

ClassClown winks. "I call this one 'The Flying Monkey Disaster!'" He pretends to trip and almost falls off the roof, but the crew's laughter fills the forest.

Suddenly, Glitch joins the dance circle, busting out a series of breakdancing moves—spinning on his head and popping back up with a flourish. Even Tactix, usually serious and composed, surprises everyone with a precise, robotic dance.

Swizzler doubles over with laughter. "Didn't know you had it in you, Tactix!"

Trekka adds to the fun, belting out the lyrics to the song almost as loud as the music itself. Her voice carries surprisingly well, making the whole crew pause to listen for a moment before joining in.

As the music winds down, everyone's catching their breath, smiling and panting from the dance party.

Swizzler wipes the sweat from his brow, grinning from ear to ear. "Alright, enough dancing. For my real birthday wish, I want to master wall climbing. Think you guys can help me out?"

The crew exchanges a determined look, already gearing up for their next challenge. "Let's do it," Cooked says, clapping his hands together. "This is going to be your best birthday yet."

The crew gathers at the base of the towering cliff wall in the Forest map, their favorite spot for practicing new skills. Swizzler steps forward, looking up with determination in his eyes. "I've been trying to figure this out forever," he admits, rubbing his palms together nervously. "If I can master wall climbing today, it'll be the best birthday gift ever."

Cooked, the fearless leader of the group, grins at him. "You've got this, Swizzler. We're going to teach you the CEO techniques of wall climbing today. By the end of this, you'll be scaling walls like a pro."

Glitch steps in, nodding in agreement. "It's all about momentum and control. Wall climbing isn't just about getting up—it's about using the walls themselves to keep you moving higher."

Tactix takes his usual strategic stance, pointing to the crease where the two walls meet. "Alright, let's break this down step by step," he says. "The first thing you need to do is get close to the wall—really close. It's easier if you start right where the two walls form a crease."

Swizzler nods, stepping up to the crease, his hand hovering near the wall. "Okay, what's next?"

Cooked demonstrates by placing his hand flat against the wall. "The key is to get your palm flat against the surface. Make sure your hand isn't clipping into the wall—your monke palm needs to be completely parallel to it," he explains. "Tilt your hand slightly so that your fingers are pointing towards the crease. This helps with control and makes it easier to push yourself off."

Swizzler places his hand against the wall, feeling the grip. He moves his arm down, pulling himself slightly upward. "Whoa, I'm sticking to the wall!" he exclaims.

Glitch nods. "Exactly! When your hand is flat against the wall, it creates a brief moment of 'stickiness' where you can hold your position before gravity kicks in. Practice that a few times—get used to the feeling of your hand sticking before you push off."

Griddy steps up, eager to try. She slaps her hand on the wall and slides down with a laugh. "Well, I'm great at sticking for about half a second!" she jokes.

Tactix smiles encouragingly. "Don't worry, Griddy. That's how it starts. Just keep practicing the hand placement and feel the wall grip."

Cooked continues, demonstrating the next move. "Now, instead of pulling yourself directly up, you're going to push yourself into the wall on the other side of the crease. Think of it like you're bouncing back and forth, like a ping pong ball."

Glitch chimes in, showing Swizzler the motion. He places his hand on one wall, pushes into the crease, and bounces off to the opposite side. "The trick is not to push yourself away from the wall," Glitch explains. "Push into it, aiming towards the other wall. It's more of a diagonal push than a straight jump."

Swizzler watches carefully, nodding as he mimics the move. He pushes himself off one wall and lands his hand on the other side, but he pushes too hard and loses his balance, bouncing back to the ground.

"Easy there, Swizzler!" Trekka calls out, laughing. "You don't want to launch yourself into orbit. It's all about gentle, controlled pushes."

Swizzler grins, wiping his brow. "Got it—more finesse, less power."

Cooked looks up at the cliff, demonstrating a full climb. He starts at the bottom, bouncing quickly back and forth between the two walls, gaining height with each push. "This is the 'ping pong' method," he says, scaling the wall with ease. "You want to bounce from one wall to the other, keeping your body close. The moment you start pushing away from the wall, you'll lose your momentum and fall."

Swizzler takes a deep breath and tries again. He places his hand flat, pushes off, and bounces back and forth, making it halfway up before sliding back down. "I almost had it!" he shouts, his voice a mix of frustration and excitement.

Tactix steps in, giving a thumbs up. "You're getting it, Swizzler. Just remember to keep your body angled towards the wall. It's not a race—focus on each move."

Griddy, determined as ever, joins in the practice. She slides down repeatedly, but she never loses her smile. "I'm becoming a pro at gliding down gracefully!" she jokes, making everyone laugh.

Trekka stands by her side, offering encouragement. "You're actually getting better, Griddy. Each time you're sticking a little longer. Don't give up—you'll get there."

Cooked watches Swizzler attempt the climb again. "Wall climbing is one of the toughest skills in Gorilla Tag," he says to the group. "It's not something you master in a day. It takes practice, patience, and a lot of failed attempts. But every time you stick just a little longer, you're making progress."

Swizzler nods, taking a deep breath and trying once more. He focuses, moving slower, sticking each hand against the wall and bouncing back and forth. This time, he makes it three-quarters of the way up before slipping. He lands on the ground, but instead of frustration, there's a huge smile on his face.

"I almost made it!" Swizzler shouts triumphantly. The crew erupts into cheers.

"You did great, Swizzler!" Griddy exclaims. "You're getting better every time."

Glitch claps him on the back. "See? Told you you'd get it. Now, it's just a matter of practicing until you can do it without thinking."

Swizzler beams, looking at the crew around him. "This has been the best birthday ever. Thanks for helping me out, guys."

The crew sprawls out around the picnic table, catching their breath and laughing about the day's antics. The sun dips lower in the sky, casting long, golden shadows through the Forest as the group settles into a moment of comfortable silence.

ClassClown breaks the quiet, leaning back and stretching his arms. "You know, I think I pulled a muscle doing that crazy dance," he groans, rubbing his shoulder with exaggerated drama. "I might need a professional to check this out."

"This was seriously the best day we've had in a long time," Cooked says, stretching his arms with a big smile. "Thanks for making it unforgettable, everyone."

Griddy snickers, shaking her head. "You definitely need help, but not the kind you're thinking of."

Tactix smirks, leaning forward. "I've got to admit, ClassClown, your moves were something else. I didn't know you could make falling look like a dance move."

ClassClown gasps, feigning offense. "It's called creative expression, Tactix. You wouldn't understand— it's an art form."

Swizzler grins, adjusting his new party hat. "Well, if

it's an art form, then I'm lucky to have witnessed a masterpiece today," he jokes, giving ClassClown a playful nudge.

Trekka chimes in, still humming along to the music Griddy had played earlier. "The only thing better than our dance-off was seeing Swizzler finally nail that wall climb," she says, raising a fist in celebration.

Swizzler's face lights up, his gratitude evident. "I've been trying to get the hang of that for ages. I couldn't have done it without all of you cheering me on. Seriously, you guys made this birthday the best one yet."

Cooked gives him a thumbs-up, his expression warm. "That's what friends are for. We've all grown so much together, and today just proved it."

Glitch, leaning casually against the table, adds with a smile, "You know, I've played a lot of games and met a lot of monke's, but this crew? You're something special."

Griddy jumps up, her energy still high despite the long day. "Alright, before we all log off, how about one last selfie to remember this epic day?"

The group huddles together, putting on their silliest faces as ClassClown snaps the shot. "Perfect!" he exclaims. "That one's going on the wall of fame."

Cooked gets up, stretching his arms. "Alright, everyone. Same time tomorrow?"

"Same time, *new code*," Trekka corrects him with a grin. "Let's switch it up—something special. How about we call it *DanceFloor*?"

The crew nods in agreement, their trust and friendship stronger than ever. As they begin logging off one by one, Swizzler gives a final wave. "See you all tomorrow. Thanks again for everything, guys. You're the best."

The Forest fades as they log off, but the laughter and joy of their day lingers, a reminder of just how far they've come and the adventures still waiting ahead.

8 BYTE'S ULTIMATUM

The crew logs into their new room code, DanceFloor, the name already putting a smile on everyone's face. The Forest map feels fresh with the morning sunlight streaming through the treetops, and the atmosphere is light-hearted as they laugh about yesterday's antics.

"This code is perfect," Trekka says, hopping onto a branch. "It's got good vibes all over it."

Cooked grins, stretching his arms. "Alright, team. Let's make today about fun—no drama, no chaos. Just the way we like it."

But their laughter cuts short as a dull grey gorilla emerges from the shadows at the edge of the map. Byte's cosmetics match his unremarkable personality, but the arrogance in his voice makes him stand out like a sore thumb.

"Well, well," Byte sneers, his voice dripping with sarcasm. "Look who's pretending to be a crew. And here I thought Glitch had some standards."

Glitch visibly stiffens, his cheerful demeanor replaced by discomfort. "Byte, what are you doing here?"

Byte smirks, leaning against a tree. "Oh, you know,

just checking out the competition. Can't let you have all the fun without me, Glitch." He pauses, eyeing the rest of the group. "Or should I say, your new... team."

ClassClown tries to break the tension with humor. "Uh, do we charge rent for uninvited guests? Because this guy seems like a freeloader."

Griddy giggles nervously, but the atmosphere remains heavy.

"Seriously, Byte," Cooked says firmly, stepping forward. "We didn't invite you, and this is a private room. What's your deal?"

Byte shrugs nonchalantly. "I heard your little code at school and thought I'd drop by. After all, Glitch and I go way back, don't we?" His eyes narrow at Glitch. "You traded up for this crew? Thought you'd want to roll with the best, not these noobs."

Glitch's fists clench, but before he can respond, Byte adds, "Tell you what—why don't I show you all what a real player looks like? Let's play a game. Or are you all too scared to lose?"

The crew exchanges uneasy glances, the tension rising. Trekka whispers, "This guy's bad news."

Cooked steps up, his tone calm but commanding. "Alright, Byte. You want to play? Let's see what you've got. But remember—this is our room, and we play by our rules."

Byte grins, his dull grey form now a looming presence in the vibrant Forest. "Oh, this is going to be fun."

As the crew prepares for Byte's proposed challenge, Glitch mutters under his breath, "You don't know what you've just started, Byte."

Byte smirks, pacing in front of the crew as if sizing them up. "Alright, listen up, amateurs," he says, his tone dripping with arrogance. "We're playing King of the Branch. Simple rules: first one to the highest branch wins.

No resets, no excuses."

Trekka narrows her eyes. "Why do I feel like this isn't going to be fun?"

Byte ignores her, turning his gaze to Glitch. "What do you say, old pal? Show me if your shiny new crew is worth anything."

Glitch hesitates, glancing at the group. "Byte, this isn't—"

"Oh, come on," Byte interrupts. "What's the matter? Afraid they'll see what real skill looks like?" His words are laced with venom, but his grin never wavers.

Cooked steps in, crossing his arms. "We're not afraid of you, Byte. Let's do this."

The group exchanges uneasy glances, clearly picking up on Byte's bad intentions, but they agree. The energy shifts as they take their starting positions at the base of the Forest's central tree, the highest in the map.

"Ready, set... go!" Byte shouts, launching himself into the air.

The crew scrambles upward, swinging and climbing with everything they've got. Trekka and Griddy take the lower branches, moving cautiously but steadily. Cooked and Tactix race to the middle, strategizing their paths.

Byte, however, is anything but strategic. He barrels through, shoving anyone in his way. "Outta my way, noobs!" he yells, swiping at ClassClown, who barely hangs onto his branch.

"Hey, watch it!" ClassClown protests, his voice tinged with frustration. "It's just a game, dude!"

"To me, it's a win," Byte fires back, already scaling past Cooked with a reckless burst of speed.

Glitch clenches his jaw, his usual playful demeanor replaced by a steely resolve. He glances down at Tactix. "Keep everyone steady. I've got him."

The branches shake as Byte climbs higher, taunting

the crew below. "Is this really the best you've got, Glitch? Guess I was right to move on."

Cooked, not one to back down, pushes harder, matching Byte's pace. "You're not winning this, Byte," he calls out, his voice firm. "Not today."

The Forest fills with the sound of crushing leaves and heavy breathing as the tension mounts. Griddy slips slightly but regains her position, calling out, "We're still in this, guys! Don't let him get to you!"

Byte reaches the final stretch, a smirk plastered across his face. But just as he reaches for the highest branch, Glitch swings in from the side with a perfectly timed move, blocking Byte's path.

"Not so fast," Glitch says coldly.

The crew cheers from below as Byte's smirk falters. But the game isn't over yet, and Byte's frustration is about to boil over.

Byte grips the branch, glaring at Glitch. "Fine. Let's make it more interesting," he growls. Before anyone can react, Byte activates a menu and triggers a new mode. The familiar sound of an Infection Mode alert rings out across the map, and the Forest begins to shift ominously.

The sound of the Infection Mode alert pierces the Forest, cutting through the crew's shouts. The atmosphere shifts as red-tinted light pulses faintly through the trees, signaling the start of the chaotic new mode.

"What just happened?" Trekka asks, looking around in confusion.

Byte leans casually against a branch, grinning like he's just pulled the ultimate prank. "Oh, didn't I mention? I triggered Double Trouble Infection Mode. Twice the fun, twice the chaos." He lets out a low chuckle, his eyes glinting with mischief. "Let's see if your little crew can handle it."

Cooked glares at Byte. "You're unbelievable."

"Thanks for the compliment," Byte replies smugly. He turns to Glitch. "What do you say, Glitch? Join forces with me, and we'll show these amateurs what real skill looks like."

Glitch doesn't respond immediately, his expression unreadable. Byte raises an eyebrow. "Come on, old buddy. Don't tell me you're actually enjoying this noob parade."

"Cut it out, Byte," Glitch finally says, his voice firm. "I'm with them."

Byte's grin falters for a fraction of a second before he recovers. "Suit yourself," he sneers. "Guess I'll just have to do this solo."

The game begins with Byte and the AI-designated second infected as the starters. The crew scatters, their earlier camaraderie giving way to focused urgency as they race to adapt.

"Tactix, what's the plan?" Cooked asks as he leaps to a higher branch.

Tactix's voice is calm but commanding. "Spread out but stay within visual range of at least one person. Use the double walls to keep moving, and don't let them corner you."

Byte, meanwhile, is reveling in the chaos. He chases Trekka with reckless abandon, intentionally making loud stomping sounds to throw her off. "Run, Trekka, run!" he jeers. "Bet you can't outlast me!"

Griddy, hanging precariously from a low branch, shouts, "Leave her alone, Byte!"

"Oh, I'll get to you next," Byte snaps, turning his attention to her. "You're all just warm-ups."

Swizzler narrowly avoids a tag by vaulting to a higher platform. "He's playing dirty," he calls out. "This isn't about the game—it's about making us look bad."

Tactix nods, watching Byte's erratic movements. "Exactly. He's trying to throw us off our game—and each other. Don't fall for it."

The crew works together to evade Byte and the AI-infected, but the pressure mounts as the infected duo gains ground. Byte's taunts grow louder and more pointed.

"Glitch, you really traded this for me?" Byte yells, swinging after him. "Biggest L of your life, buddy."

Glitch finally snaps, pausing mid-swing to glare at Byte. "The only L here is you, Byte," he fires back. "Now stop acting like a sore loser and play fair."

Byte laughs, a hollow, humorless sound. "Fair? Where's the fun in that?"

Despite Byte's antics, the crew holds their ground, relying on their skills and teamwork to keep the infected at bay. Tactix's calls keep them coordinated, Cooked leads daring escapes, and even Griddy manages to stay one step ahead of the chaos.

But Byte's relentless aggression begins to wear on them. The crew knows they need to do more than just survive—they need to outsmart Byte at his own game.

Cooked lands on a branch near Glitch, whispering urgently. "We need a plan to shut this down. Byte's trying to break us apart, but we're not giving him the satisfaction." Glitch nods, determination flashing in his eyes. "Let's show him what teamwork really looks like."

Cooked, perched on a mid-level branch, raises his hand to signal a pause. His voice cuts through the scattered chatter, firm and resolute. "Hold up, everyone. Byte, we need to talk."

The crew gathers below, glancing between Cooked and Byte, their expressions a mixture of curiosity and tension. Byte stays where he is, lazily leaning against a tree trunk, spinning his dull grey party balloon idly. His smirk oozes arrogance. "What's the matter, Cooked? Can't handle the heat?"

Cooked's expression hardens, but his tone remains measured. "This isn't about the game, Byte. It's about respect. We came here to have fun, not to deal with someone tearing us down."

Griddy nods from her perch nearby, her usually bubbly demeanor tinged with frustration. "Yeah, Byte. You're sucking all the fun out of this."

Swizzler chimes in, arms crossed. "You don't need to win by making everyone else feel small."

Tactix, ever the voice of reason, steps forward, his gaze steady. "Byte, we get that you're competitive. But if you want to play with us, it's got to be on our terms. No bullying, no toxic comments, and no trying to divide us."

Byte's smirk falters briefly, but he quickly recovers, shrugging dismissively. "You're all so sensitive. It's just a game. Glitch used to get it. What happened, buddy?"

All eyes turn to Glitch, who's been uncharacteristically quiet. Slowly, he steps forward, his expression serious. "What happened, Byte, is that I've moved on. This crew? They're everything you're not—fun, supportive, and actually here for the right reasons."

Byte's smug mask cracks, revealing a flicker of hurt beneath his arrogance. "Oh, I see how it is," he sneers, his voice dripping with bitterness. "Trading loyalty for laughs, huh? Don't come crying back when this little 'crew' gets smashed."

Cooked shakes his head. "This isn't about sides, Byte. It's about boundaries. And we're setting ours."

For a moment, Byte doesn't move, his gaze darting between the crew. Then he lets out a short, hollow laugh. "Fine. Have it your way. But don't think this is the end." He points a finger at Glitch, his voice low and menacing. "You'll see. Shadow and Trollz were just the beginning."

With that, Byte powers off his headset, his avatar disappearing into thin air.

The crew lets out a collective breath, the tension dissolving like mist. Trekka breaks the silence with a nervous laugh. "Well, that was... intense."

Cooked smiles, a mix of relief and pride. "We stood up for ourselves. That's what matters."

Griddy hops down from her branch, beaming. "And we didn't let him ruin the game. Win-win!"

The group agrees to keep playing, their energy lighter and more focused now. Before logging out, they decide on a new room code. "Let's call it Alliance," Tactix suggests. "It means strength through unity."

The crew logs out, but the camaraderie they've built stays with them. As Cooked removes his headset, he feels a renewed sense of pride in their group. Byte may have left, but the bond they share has only grown stronger.

Cooked leans back in his chair, an obstinate grin on his face. "Bring it on, Byte. We're ready for whatever's next."

9 INVASION OF BAD CODE

The crew logged into their new private room, Alliance, with an air of excitement and relief. The Forest map stretched out before them, bathed in the familiar glow of late-afternoon sunlight. Birds chirped, leaves swirled, and the iconic central tree stood tall and proud, like the crew's unwavering bond.

"Ah, Alliance," Trekka said, taking in the view. "Feels good, doesn't it? No Byte, no Trollz, no Shadow, no Cringe. Just us."

"Finally," Cooked agreed, spinning in place to stretch his virtual arms. "Fresh code, fresh start. What's the plan today, Glitch?"

Glitch, standing near the treehouse, grinned. "I've got something cool lined up—a new game I've been working on. Think you're ready for it?"

ClassClown flopped dramatically onto the ground. "As long as it doesn't involve wall climbing again. My arms still feel like floppy noodles."

The group laughed, their camaraderie easing into a

playful rhythm. But as Griddy was about to make another joke, something strange caught her eye.

"Hey, is it just me, or did that branch just... flicker?" she asked, pointing to a tree limb in the distance.

The laughter died down as everyone turned to look. The branch wavered, its texture shimmering like a mirage before snapping back into place.

"That's... weird," Tactix said, squinting his eyes. "I've never seen that happen previously."

Before anyone could respond, more distortions began rippling through the Forest. Branches shifted unnaturally, the ground below pulsed between solid textures and empty voids, and the sky overhead shimmered, as though someone had pressed pause on reality and was now struggling to resume the game.

"What's going on?" Swizzler asked, his voice tinged with unease. "Glitch, is this part of your game?"

Glitch's grin faded as he scanned the map, his eyes I disbelief. "No. This isn't me. This is... something else."

The crew froze as the map suddenly locked in place, the familiar sounds of the Forest replaced by a hollow, mechanical hum. A bright red gorilla materialized on the central platform, his vivid color cutting through the muted tones of the corrupted map.

"Noob alert!" the red gorilla sneered, his voice dripping with mockery. "Welcome to my Forest. You must be the famous crew I've been hearing so much about."

"Who are you?" Cooked demanded, stepping forward, his fists clenched.

The gorilla laughed, the sound cold and unnerving. "The name's Zero. And this is just the beginning."

The crew exchanged nervous glances as Zero's bright

red frame seemed to pulse, his presence a menacing beacon in the glitching map. Whatever was happening, it was clear: Alliance wasn't safe after all.

The crew barely had time to process Zero's arrival when more figures materialized around him. Brightly red gorillas, their forms unnervingly distorted with bulging muscles and jagged edges, surrounded the platform. Each one radiated an aura of hostility, their expressions twisted into mocking grins.

"Allow me to introduce my crew," Zero said with a sweeping gesture. "We're the Hackers, and this is our playground now."

"What do you want?" Trekka demanded, her voice steady despite the unease creeping into the group.

"Want?" Zero repeated with a laugh. "I want to show you what happens when amateurs meddle where they don't belong. You've been making waves—Shadow, Trollz, Byte… they were just the warm-up."

Before anyone could respond, Zero clapped his hands, and the Forest map shimmered violently. The ground beneath them moved like water, branches bent and twisted unnaturally, and the sky darkened as though a storm were about to break.

Cooked tried to move but stumbled, his usual smooth motions slowed as if he were wading through quicksand. "What's happening?" he shouted.

"Welcome to our world," one of the Hackers snarled. "Let's see you climb now."

Griddy reached for a branch to steady herself, but her hand slid off as though the wood were coated in slippery substance. She fell back to the ground with a frustrated cry. "I can't grip anything! It's like everything's made of slime!"

Above them, platforms and branches flickered in and out of existence. Tactix attempted to leap to a nearby branch, only for it to vanish mid-air, sending him tumbling to the ground. "This isn't a game—it's a trap," he snarled.

Zero's laughter echoed through the distorted map. "Oh, it's still a game. Just not one you're equipped to play."

Swizzler, always quick on his feet, tried darting towards the treehouse, but the terrain shifted beneath him, sending him sliding into a void that reappeared as solid ground just before he fell through. "They're controlling everything!" he shouted. "We can't outmaneuver them."

Meanwhile, from the shadows, Byte watched silently. His dull grey form blended into the chaos, his expression unreadable. But when one of the Hackers landed a perfectly timed tag on ClassClown, Byte allowed himself a small, vindictive smile. He didn't need to join in; watching the crew struggle was satisfying enough.

"Why are you doing this?" Glitch shouted, his voice cutting through the noise.

Zero turned his glowing red gaze to him. "Because we can," he said simply. "And because I don't like competition. You thought you were special? A crew like yours doesn't belong here."

Cooked struggled to get up, his fists clenched. "We're not giving up. Whatever you're trying to prove, you won't break us."

"Oh, but I already have," Zero said, his grin widening. "This is just the beginning."

The Forest was no longer their familiar playground. Every step was treacherous, every jump an act of faith.

Branches shimmered and faltered, disappearing just as they reached for them. The usual rustling leaves and bird chirps were replaced by a low, distorted hum that seemed to vibrate in their bones.

Cooked gathered the crew beneath the central tree, his expression grim but determined. "We stick together," he said firmly, his voice cutting through the rising panic. "That's the only way we'll make it out of this."

But before anyone could respond, the ground beneath them trembled violently. Cracks of black void snaked outward, and sections of the Forest floor dissolved into a swirling abyss. The distorted hum grew louder, resonating like a warning siren. Screams erupted as the crew stumbled backward, the abyss seeming to reach for them.

"Move!" Tactix shouted, his usual calm replaced by urgency. "Head for the double walls and onto the platform near it. We can regroup there and figure out their pattern!" His voice wavered as the ground beneath them rippled like water, throwing off their footing. Each step felt unstable, the world around them glitching uncontrollably. Tactix's strategy sounded solid, but with the Forest itself turning against them, their chances seemed to grow slimmer with every passing second.

Glitch, meanwhile, was scanning the distorted environment, his sharp eyes catching glimpses of code-like patterns rippling across the surfaces. "This isn't random," he muttered. "They're controlling everything—movement speed, grip, the map's integrity. There's got to be a weak spot."

"Glitch, we don't have time to analyze!" Cooked shouted as a branch voided out of existence, sending him tumbling to the ground. He scrambled back up, but the slippery surface made it impossible to gain traction. "We're sitting ducks here!"

Above them, Zero perched on a high branch, his red form glowing menacingly in the dim light. His voice rang out, mocking and loud. "What's the matter? Your big plans not working? Maybe I should slow things down even more—give you noobs a chance."

Another Hacker lunged from the shadows, tagging ClassClown. His monke's coat turned a sickly shade of red, and with a distorted laugh, the Hacker sneered, "Out you go." ClassClown vanished, his avatar disintegrating into a cascade of broken polygons before being kicked out of the room.

"ClassClown's gone!" Griddy cried, panic rising in her voice. "We're getting picked off one by one!"

Swizzler slipped on the glitching ground, narrowly avoiding another Hacker. "We can't run, and we can't climb! What do we do, Cooked?"

Cooked hesitated, trying to think of a strategy that could turn the tide. But every plan he considered fell apart under the weight of the Hackers' control. "We need to hold our ground," he said finally. "Find somewhere stable and make them come to us."

Glitch shook his head, his expression tight. "No, that won't work. They'll just erase the ground under us. We need to disrupt their control somehow."

Zero laughed from above, his tone drenched with arrogance. "Disrupt our control? Oh, that's adorable. You don't even understand what you're dealing with."

Another Hacker leapt at Trekka, tagging her with a brutal swipe of its oversized hand. Her avatar dissolved in a cascade of distorted pixels as she let out a frustrated shout, disappearing from the game.

Just before her voice cut off entirely, a chilling, mechanical whisper slipped through the air, audible to everyone still in the room: "One more down. Who's next?"

The crew froze, the weight of the ominous message settling over them like the chilling presence of a Skinwalker lurking just out of sight, its unnatural stillness impossible to shake. The echo of the Hacker's distorted words lingered, twisting through their minds, feeding the rising fear like a darkness that refuses to fade.

With each fallen teammate, the weight of defeat bore down on the remaining crew. Cooked's fists clenched and pounded on his chest with anger bubbling at the surface as he watched his friend and sister vanish before his eyes. From the next room, he could hear her grief spilling over in real life, sharp and raw.

This was personal now.

"I've had enough," he roared through clenched teeth, his voice low but charged with fury. "You don't mess with family."

But even as he spoke, the crew's movements grew more sluggish, their options dwindling. Griddy attempted to branch to safety, only to slip and land in the clutches of another Hacker.

The Hacker leaned close to her avatar, its distorted, glitching face a grotesque mockery of a smile. "Run all you want," it rasped, its voice crackling with static. "There's nowhere to hide in our world."

Griddy's scream of frustration was the last thing they heard before she disappeared in a swirl of corrupted pixels, leaving only Cooked, Glitch, and Tactix to face the nightmare unraveling around them.

The Forest was no longer a familiar playground; it was

a warzone consumed by anarchy. Cooked, Glitch, and Tactix were left shook, their every move hampered by the distorted, slippery terrain. The glow of the Hackers' bright red forms circled them, taunting and relentless.

"Stick together," Cooked commanded, his voice steady despite the weight of the situation. "We've faced worse." But deep down, he knew this was different.

Glitch tried to climb a tree for higher ground, but the trunk dissolved beneath his hands, sending him tumbling back to the corrupted ground. A Hacker materialized beside him, its towering form casting a shadow over his avatar. "Stay down, traitor," it hissed, tagging him with a sharp jab.

Glitch's avatar sparked as he began to vanish. "I'll figure this out," he said, his voice laced with both determination and regret. "You guys…just survive." He disappeared in a burst of static, leaving Cooked and Tactix to face the relentless Hackers alone.

Tactix, ever the strategist, attempted to guide Cooked to a safer area. "There's a pattern to their moves. If we can—" His words were cut off as a Hacker lunged from the shadows, dragging him down.

Tactix's voice echoed as he was erased. "Cooked, you're the leader for a reason. You can do this. Don't give up!"

Now alone, Cooked clenched his fists, staring down the trio of Hackers who circled him like predators. The ground beneath him unstable and twisted, transforming into quicksand that pulled at his body, anchoring him in place.

"You've been warned, leader," one of the Hackers sneered, its robotic voice saturated with malice. "Next time, it won't just be a game."

Cooked fought to the last moment, struggling against the sinking ground. The Hackers' mocking laughter surrounded him, their voices overlapping in a cacophony of cruelty. "Your crew is finished," one spat. "You'll never stand against us."

As the quicksand swallowed him, Cooked let out a frustrated roar. "This isn't over," he declared, his voice cutting through their taunts. But his avatar dissolved, leaving the Forest eerily silent of the once playful crew.

Back in the real world, Cooked sat at his desk, his headset still in his hands. He stared at it as if it might come to life on its own. A notification pinged on his screen—a group chat from the crew. He clicked it immediately.

Cooked: "Everyone okay? That was insane."

Tactix: "Define 'okay.' I feel like I just got kicked out of reality."

Griddy: "My hands are still shaking. What even was that?"

Trekka: "Do you think our headsets are… infected or something? Those glitches felt too real."

A tense pause hung in the chat as if no one wanted to voice the growing fear. Finally, Glitch chimed in.

Glitch: "I don't think it's your headsets. This is bigger than that. These Hackers… they're not just messing around. I've seen this kind of code before. It's designed to manipulate the game at its core."

Swizzler: "So what does that mean? Are we just done playing Gorilla Tag?"

Glitch hesitated, his usual confidence faltering. "No. We're not done. But if we want to fight back, we need to figure out how they're doing this. I'll dig deeper and see what I can find. But…"

Cooked: "But what?"

Glitch's next message came through slowly, like he was typing it one letter at a time. "I don't know if we'll win this one."

The chat went silent. No jokes, no playful banter. Just a creeping sense that their crew wasn't safe—not in the game, and maybe not even in real life.

Cooked finally broke the silence. "We've made it through everything else. We'll figure this out. Meet tomorrow—same time, new code."

Griddy: "What's the new code?"

Cooked's fingers hovered over his keyboard before typing: "Firewall."

But as he hit send, a notification popped up. A single, ominous message from an unknown user:

"You think a new code will save you? Think again."

Cooked stared at the screen, his resolve hardening. "Tomorrow, we take this fight to them."

10 FIREWALL

IRL the crew gathered at the skate park; their usual laughter replaced by a tense purpose. Cooked paced back and forth, his fists clenching at his sides. The memory of his sister and crew being ruthlessly erased from the Forest replayed in his mind. He stopped abruptly, looking at the others.

"This isn't just about us getting kicked out of a game," Cooked said, his voice steady but simmering with anger. "What they did was personal. They crossed a line, and we need to show them we won't back down."

Griddy, sitting cross-legged on the edge of the skate ramp, nodded. "But how do we fight back against people like that? They're in the game, outside of it—they're everywhere."

"We start with the basics," Tactix interjected. "We report them the second they log in. Moderators can't ignore all of us."

Glitch leaned against his scooter; his normally confident expression tinged with unease. "Strength in numbers will help in-game, but there's more at stake. Byte and those Hackers could've tampered with our headsets. If they planted malware or a worm, our accounts—maybe even our devices—could be compromised."

"That's why we're leaving our phones behind," Trekka added. "No chance for them to eavesdrop on this plan."

ClassClown attempted to lighten the mood, kicking his skateboard up into his hands. "I say we get in there, report them like maniacs, and hope for the best. Worst case, we need a new game."

Cooked shot him a glare but softened slightly. "This is our game, ClassClown. We're not letting anyone take it from us."

Trekka broke the tension with a thoughtful nod. "We'll use the Firewall code. But once we report them, we have to think ahead. What's the next move if they come back? We need a long-term strategy."

The crew exchanged persevering glances, the resolve in their eyes unspoken but clear. Cooked clapped his hands together. "Alright, let's do this. Meet online in thirty minutes. And remember: stick to the plan."

As they dispersed, Trekka called out, "Whatever happens, we handle it together."

Cooked, the last to leave with his sister by his side, looked back at the empty skate park, his jaw set. "Together," he repeated under his breath, a quiet promise to protect his crew and make things right.

The crew logged into the private room Firewall, the impact of their earlier discussion lingering. The Forest map appeared around them, its usual serenity seeming slightly off, like a calm before the storm. Each member moved cautiously, scanning the area for signs of trouble as they made their way to the leaderboard.

"Alright, everyone, positions," Cooked commanded, his tone serious. The crew gathered near the leaderboard, forming a semi-circle. "If the Hackers show up, you know what to do. No hesitation."

Glitch nodded, his silver avatar sparkling with the darkness. "Remember, the more of us that report them at once, the higher the chance moderators will respond quickly. Strength in numbers."

"I still think we should've named the code StrengthInNumbers," ClassClown quipped, attempting to lighten the mood. "Firewall's cool and all, but come on, it's a missed opportunity."

Griddy smirked. "Just focus on the mission, clown. We can debate room codes after we save the game."

To keep up appearances, the crew began practicing wall climbing and branching near the leaderboard. Trekka led the way, her agile movements smooth as she darted from one branch to another. "This spot's perfect for branching drills," she said, dropping down to help Griddy. "Keep your momentum going—don't overthink it."

Griddy huffed, attempting the move and slipping back down. "I'm trying! These walls are slipperier than ClassClown's jokes."

"Hey, my jokes are solid!" ClassClown protested, dramatically pretending to stumble off a branch. "See? Comedy gold."

Despite the tension, laughter broke out, their camaraderie briefly lightening the mood. Cooked leaned against the leaderboard, watching his friends. "This is what they're trying to take from us," he said softly. "Not just the game—but this."

The team grew quiet, the reality of the situation settling in again. Tactix cleared his throat, breaking the silence. "Keep your focus. They'll show up when we least expect it."

Glitch adjusted his position, keeping a careful eye on the map. "They will show up. It's just a matter of time. And when they do, we'll be ready."

The lighthearted banter dissipated as the crew's willpower solidified. Every creak of the branches, every faint rustle of leaves, heightened their anticipation. They knew what was at stake, and they weren't about to let the Hackers win without a fight.

The Forest map darkened unnaturally as the crew waited near the leaderboard, their nerves taut. Then it happened—an aberration in the air, a ripple across the ground, and branches shifting as if alive. A streak of lightening arced through the sky, followed by the unmistakable arrival of the Hacker trio.

Zero stood at the forefront, his bright red figure towering over the map, his bulky avatar glitching at the edges. Behind him, the other two Hackers loomed, their robotic, distorted forms pulsing with energy. Their presence was oppressive, each movement sending shockwaves through the environment.

"Well, well, look who decided to show up," Zero said, his voice tainted with mockery. His red avatar took a step forward, and the ground beneath him rippled like liquid. "Did you really think a little private room code could keep us out?"

Branches wavered, disappearing and reappearing unpredictably. The leaderboard itself shimmered, but the report buttons remained intact—a small glimmer of hope.

"Do it now!" Cooked yelled, pointing to the buttons. The crew sprang into action, racing toward the leaderboard. Griddy and Trekka reached it first, their hands slamming down on the buttons with urgency.

Zero, unbothered, laughed as he advanced. "Do you think banning us will stop us? We always find our way back. This game belongs to us."

The other Hackers moved to block the crew, their distorted forms glitching ominously. Tactix darted around one of them, narrowly avoiding a swipe. "Keep going!" he shouted. "We have to do this together!"

Glitch sprinted to the buttons, his silver color blending with the chaos. "Don't let up! Every report counts!" he urged.

The Hackers retaliated, their tactics turning desperate. One moment, Trekka found herself on solid ground; the next, the branch beneath her vanished, sending her sprawling. She scrambled up, shaking off her frustration, and hit the button again.

Cooked, his determination unwavering, tackled one of the Hackers to create an opening. "Go! Hit the button!" he roared, his voice cutting through the mayhem.

ClassClown, for once serious, stood his ground beside Griddy. "They're not stopping us," he said, slamming the button repeatedly. "Not this time."

Zero's mocking tone wavered as he realized the crew's persistence. "You think you've won? You can't get rid of us. Not permanently." He lunged toward the leaderboard, but it was too late.

A sudden jolt shook the map. The Hackers' forms flickered erratically as the moderators intervened. One by one, the trio was booted from the game, their avatars dissolving into fragmented pixels.

As the map stabilized, the crew collapsed near the leaderboard, their breaths coming in ragged gasps. Cooked glanced at the now-quiet Forest, his fists still clenched. "We did it—for now."

But the air still felt oppressive, the threat far from over.

As the final Hacker dissolved into jagged pixels, the Forest map stabilized, its eerie distortions fading into a fragile stillness. The familiar flutter of leaves and chirping of birds returned, but the sense of normalcy felt thin, like a brittle layer over something darker.

The crew huddled near the leaderboard, their faces a mix of relief and unease. Cooked was the first to break the silence. "They're gone—for now," he said, his voice tense with frustration. "But you heard what Zero said. They'll be back."

Tactix nodded, his analytical mind already at work. "And they weren't bluffing. If they've hacked into our private room codes, who's to say they haven't messed with our headsets too? We might be dealing with more than just in-game glitches."

Griddy's face paled. "You mean... like a virus? In our headsets?" Her voice wavered, the fear in it palpable. "What if it spreads? What if it wipes our data—or worse, bans us?"

Trekka tried to lighten the mood, though her usual confidence was strained. "Let's not panic... yet. We should check for updates or patches when we log out, maybe do a full system scan." She glanced at Glitch. "You'd know about this kind of thing, right?"

Glitch, unusually quiet, stared at the ground, his expression troubled. "I've seen this before," he admitted.

"Hackers like them aren't just here to mess with the game. They want control. If they've embedded something into the software... we'll need to act fast."

Cooked's fists tightened. "Whatever it takes, we're not letting them win. This game means too much—to all of us."

ClassClown tried to inject some levity, though his usual humor was subdued. "Well, worst case, I guess I'll finally have time for... homework?" His attempt at a joke fell flat, the burden of the moment too heavy.

Glitch finally looked up; his usual confidence replaced with a shred of doubt. "We need to be careful—together. This isn't just a game anymore."

The crew exchanged anxious glances, the realization sinking in: their beloved game had become a battleground, and the stakes were higher than ever. The echoes of the Hackers' threats lingered in their minds like a toxic haze.

Cooked broke the silence, his voice steady despite the tension. "We've made it through every challenge so far, and we'll figure this one out too. But we're not done yet."

The group nodded in agreement, the significance of their collective commitment binding them together. They weren't sure what would come next, but one thing was clear—this fight was far from over.

With the crew gathered at the familiar picnic table, their energy subdued but their spirits beginning to rekindle. The Forest felt quieter now, the eerie presence of the Hackers replaced by a cautious calm.

Cooked leaned back against the table, looking at his friends. "We handled that better than I thought we would," he said. "But we can't let our guard down."

Tactix nodded. "Agreed. But maybe we don't need to

stay in the Forest for a while. There's a whole game out there, and I hear the City's got a lot to offer."

Griddy's eyes lit up. "Oh! I heard you can bounce super high off the platforms there! And swim—can you imagine playing tag in water? I've always wanted to try that!"

ClassClown leaned in, grinning. "Forget the platforms. We have to stop by the Fortune Teller in City first. I need to know if my destiny is to finally beat Glitch in a game."

Glitch chuckled, his confidence returning. "Not likely, ClassClown. But I'd pay to see his reaction when you ask something ridiculous."

Trekka's excitement was palpable. "City's the perfect place for exploring. Tall buildings, hidden alleyways... it's got my name written all over it. I can't wait to see what we'll discover."

Cooked stood, his expression a mix of resilience and hope. "Wherever we go next, as long as we stick together, we'll handle it."

The group exchanged nods; their bond stronger than ever despite everything they'd faced. As the sun set over the Forest, its golden light streaming through the leaves, they each knew the adventure was far from over.

Trekka glanced toward the shimmering tunnel leading out of the Forest. "Looks like our next adventure isn't far off. Let's make it unforgettable."

CONCLUSION

The crew gathered at the picnic table, their laughter and banter filling the Forest map like a breath of fresh air after the tension. Cooked leaned back again, watching his friends with a faint smile. "Remember when we used to practice pinch climbing in ArmsUp?" he said. "Feels like a lifetime ago."

"And now we've gone toe-to-toe with Shadow, Cringe, Hackers, Byte's ego, and Trollz's YouTube antics," Trekka added, spinning a balloon she'd kept from Swizzler's birthday bash. "Not to mention we picked up a pretty decent teammate along the way." She winked at Glitch, who smirked.

"Decent?" Glitch replied. "I'm carrying you noobs."

Griddy rolled her eyes. "Don't let it go to your head, Glitch. Besides, we all know I'm the real MVP." She mock-flexed her arms, earning a chorus of laughter.

The crew had grown—both in skill and friendship. They'd faced down enemies, learned to trust each other, and discovered that even when things got tough, sticking together made all the difference. It wasn't just about winning; it was about having fun, respecting each other, and making memories that would last far beyond the game.

"Speaking of fun," ClassClown began, pulling out a digital book from his inventory menu. "Have you guys seen this? It's the Gorilla Tag Joke Book by Skibidi McMonke. The guy's a legend!"

"Wait," Trekka said, her eyes lighting up. "You think he's real? Like… in the game?"

"Why not?" Swizzler chimed in, flipping through the pages. "I mean, if we met him, I bet we'd have him in stitches with our stories."

Cooked grinned. "Or he'd add a chapter just for us. 'How Not to Wall Climb: Featuring Griddy.'"

"Hey!" Griddy protested, though she couldn't keep a straight face. "At least I'm good at sliding down gracefully!"

The crew burst into laughter, their energy light and carefree. It felt good to just relax and enjoy the moment after everything they'd been through.

As the sun set over the Forest map, Glitch's tone shifted. "You know," he said, his voice quieter, "there's a lot about this game we still haven't explored. City, for example. I've heard rumors about hidden mechanics there—things even the Hackers haven't figured out."

Tactix tilted his head. "Like what?"

Glitch shrugged. "Not sure, but I've got a feeling we'll find out soon enough."

Trekka leaned forward, her explorer spirit sparking. "Tall buildings, neon lights, secret hideouts—it's got my name written all over it. City's going to be sigma."

ClassClown leaned back dramatically. "As long as we stop by the Fortune Teller booth, I'm in. I need to know if my jokes are going to land in the future."

Cooked stood up, looking around at his friends. "Whatever comes next," he said, his voice steady, "we'll face it together. We've got the skills, the crew, and most importantly, the heart. There's no map we can't conquer."

As the crew exchanged nods and grins, a sense of excitement buzzed in the air. The challenges ahead didn't seem so daunting—not when they had each other. With a final glance at the glowing Forest map, they logged off, ready to tackle City and whatever adventures awaited them next.

"New map, new challenges, same crew," Cooked said with a grin. "Let's go bananas."

Forest Escape

ABOUT THE AUTHOR

Skibidi McMonke is a self-proclaimed Gorilla Tag enthusiast, expert wall climber (on good days), and occasional prankster. Known for his love of adventure and a knack for finding the funniest moments in the most chaotic games, Skibidi has turned his virtual escapades into the Gorilla Tag Adventures series.

When he's not dodging Hackers or tagging his friends in Infection Mode, you'll find him brainstorming the next big challenge, dreaming up wild new maps, and wondering what Skibidi toilets have to do with monke's anyway.

This is his debut book in the Gorilla Tag Adventures series, with more to come—so grab your headset, find your crew, and get ready to climb to the top.

Let's go bananas! 🐵

Made in the USA
Monee, IL
29 November 2024

71571661R00069